# PUBLISHING FOR TENURE AND BEYOND

# PUBLISHING FOR TENURE AND BEYOND

Franklin H. Silverman

Westport, Connecticut
London

**Library of Congress Cataloging-in-Publication Data**

Silverman, Franklin H., 1933–
      Publishing for tenure and beyond / Franklin H. Silverman.
        p.   cm.
      Includes bibliographical references and index.
      ISBN 0–275–96390–X (alk. paper). — ISBN 0-275-96391-8 (pbk. :
alk. paper)
        1. Authorship. 2. Academic writing—United States. 3. Scholarly
publishing—United States. 4. College teachers—Tenure—United
States. I. Title.
PN146.S56      1999
808'.02—dc21     99–13526

British Library Cataloguing in Publication Data is available.

Library of Congress Catalog Card Number: 99–13526
ISBN: 0–275–96390–X
      0–275–96391–8 (pbk.)

First published in 1999

Praeger Publishers, 88 Post Road West, Westport, CT 06881
An imprint of Greenwood Publishing Group, Inc.
www.praeger.com

Printed in the United States of America

The paper used in this book complies with the
Permanent Paper Standard issued by the National
Information Standards Organization (Z39.48–1984).

10 9 8 7 6 5 4 3 2 1

# Contents

# Preface

It is difficult to win a game without having a good knowledge of its rules and strategies. Getting promoted from assistant professor to associate professor and being tenured can be viewed as a game that has both rules and strategies. This book is intended to provide college and university faculty who have a tenure-track position and graduate students who will be seeking such a position with some of the information they need to play the game successfully — that is, be promoted and tenured, survive post-tenure reviews, and receive merit salary increases. Specifically, it focuses on the rules and strategies of its scholarly publishing component, in a manner that is both practical and candid.

By viewing academic publishing as a game, I am not intending to demean it. I have been an active scholar for approximately 30 years with more than a dozen books and 125 publications in peer-reviewed journals. I also have served as associate editor for my association's research journal and the chairperson of the faculty development committee for both my department and college. I am viewing academic publishing here in this way because I have found when mentoring junior faculty that doing so makes the dynamics of the process more understandable to them.

To play a game successfully, you must understand both its unwritten rules and strategies and its written ones. Unfortunately, one might appear cynical when describing a game's unwritten ones. My goal is for this book to be as helpful as I can make it. Consequently, I did not avoid describing unwritten rules and strategies to protect myself from appearing cynical.

Although departments differ somewhat on their requirements for promotion and tenure, most have requirements pertaining to the following four areas: teaching, service, scholarly publishing, and collegiality. Although those for the collegiality might not be specified, a perceived lack of collegiality is a frequent reason for one to be denied promotion or tenure. Promotion and tenure committees, however, tend to avoid using collegiality as a reason for denying promotion and tenure for legal reasons. It is illegal to discriminate against someone on the job simply because you do not like that person. Instead, a committee will try to document some weakness in teaching, service, or research. Scholarly publishing is the most likely area for the committee to choose, particularly if a candidate's record is not exceptional. It tends to be easier to document inadequacies in scholarly productivity than it is in teaching or service. Consequently, to maximize the likelihood of winning at the tenure game, you should both behave in a manner that is unlikely to cause your colleagues to question your collegiality and strive for a publication record that clearly exceeds their minimal expectations.

I interviewed a number of experienced academic authors regarding some of the topics and issues discussed in this book. Some excerpts from these interviews are included that either augment or clarify my discussion.

Much of the information about a particular topic or issue is in the chapter that deals with it. However, there also could be information pertinent to it in other chapters. Consequently, the index is a more useful tool than the table of contents for locating information about some topics and issues.

It is impossible to give credit to the many sources from which the ideas in this book have been drawn. This book is the result of more than 30 years of involvement with scholarly writing and publishing and the tenure process as well as hundreds of hours of conversations with persons engaged in these activities, particularly members of the Text and Academic Authors Association. Thus, I cannot credit this or that idea to a specific person, but I say thank you to all whose ideas I have borrowed. Some special thanks are due to Dr. Francis Lazarus at San Diego University (a former vice president for academic affairs) and Dr. Robert Moulton, dean of the Graduate College at Lamar University, for their careful reading of the entire manuscript and helpful suggestions for improving it.

This book is intended to provide accurate information with regard to the subject matter covered; however, the author and publisher accept no responsibility for inaccuracies or omissions. The author and publisher specifically disclaim any liability, loss, or risk, whether personal, financial, or otherwise, which is incurred as a consequence, directly or indirectly, from the use or application of any of the contents of this book.

# PUBLISHING FOR TENURE AND BEYOND

# 1

# The Publishing for Tenure Game — An Overview

For most members of the profession, the real strain in the academic role arises from the fact that they are, in essence, paid to do one job, whereas the worth of their service is evaluated on the basis of how well they do another. The work assignment, for which the vast majority of professors are paid, is that of teaching. . . . When they are evaluated, however, as candidates for promotion, the evaluation is made principally in terms of their research contributions to their disciplines.

— Caplow & McGee, 1958, p. 82

To survive in academia, you are likely to have to publish. Although your job description will stress teaching, the likelihood of your receiving tenure probably will depend, in large part, on your scholarly productivity. The term "publish or perish" succinctly communicates this reality.

This book is intended for — and, in fact, I will be assuming throughout the book that you, my readers, are — assistant professors or graduate students who are planning to pursue a career in college teaching. The book is actually an open letter in which I have attempted to provide information and insights that could help you create an adequate publication record for promotion and tenure and possibly for receiving merit salary increases and for obtaining and maintaining graduate faculty status. The presentation is candid, and the recommendations are pragmatic.

I have been a full professor at two institutions for more than 20 years and a university faculty member for more than 30 years. I have had approximately 125 articles published in refereed journals and have written more than 12 academic books. I have served on the editorial boards of three international journals and as an associate editor of the American Speech-Language-Hearing Association's research journal with full responsibility for processing submitted manuscripts. I have been a member of my college's promotion and tenure committee for many years. Furthermore, through involvement with faculty development at Marquette University and with the Text and Academic Authors Association, of which I am a past president, I have served as an advisor on the subject of publishing for tenure (PFT).

## THE GAME

The process by which an assistant professor gets publications for tenure is referred to throughout this book as playing the PFT game. This game, like chess, involves competitive strategy. It has rules that must be obeyed, strategies for maximizing the likelihood of winning, and referees and umpires who enforce rules and decide winners. The referees and umpires include journal and book editors and reviewers, department chairpersons, deans, and members of promotion and tenure committees.

There are several reasons why I will be describing PFT as a game throughout this book. First, it has the characteristics of a competitive strategy game. Second, by presenting it in this way I hope to help you develop an objective attitude toward scholarly publishing — an attitude that hopefully will enable you to generate an adequate publication record for tenure.

Describing PFT as a game is not meant to demean the process but rather to make it more understandable. Playing a game without realizing that you are doing so makes losing more likely.

I am not the first, incidentally, to view scholarship as game playing. Agnew and Pyke (1975) have reported, for example, that "the ingredients of any great game can be found in science — massive effort, goals, great plays, mediocre plays, lousy plays; umpires making clear calls, judgment calls, biased calls, and of course, mistaken calls. There are prizes and penalties. You will find integrity, dignity, and deals, along with good luck and bad luck — but above all you will find commitment" (pp. vii–viii).

## WHY VIEWING PUBLISHING FOR
## TENURE AS A GAME IS HELPFUL

It only makes sense to view PFT as a game if doing so would be helpful in some way. I believe strongly that it can be helpful for junior faculty (as well as graduate students who hope someday to be assistant professors) to view PFT as game playing for the reasons described in this section.

Some junior faculty commit academic suicide. They are told when they are hired that tenure decisions are based on their record of scholarly publishing (research) as well as for teaching and service. They invest much of themselves in teaching — particularly undergraduate teaching — and often are highly rated by their students. They also are likely to volunteer for more than their fair share of student advising, committee work, and other service to the institution. They might begin projects but either never write them up for publication or never do so again after the first manuscript they submit to a journal is either rejected or not accepted as is. They might get a few publications near the end of their probationary period because of threats by their dean or department chairperson to terminate their employment before they have an opportunity to be considered for tenure. They apply for tenure in their up or out year and convince themselves that their institution will forgive their lack of publication because of their exemplary teaching record and service to their department. They genuinely are surprised when they are denied tenure.

I am assuming here and throughout the book that publishing is a requirement for tenure. This is not always true. As one of my interviewees, who is a professor at a community college, stated: "In California at least, tenure is possible at community colleges for full-time faculty after five years, although whether as a 'professor' or as an 'instructor' depends entirely on the college. The job is the same no matter what title we are given. Publication plays little or no part in tenure, as teaching is our first and foremost role." However, this interviewee indicated that there may be a publication requirement for tenure in some departments of community colleges. "In the community colleges, most instructors hold master's degrees rather than Ph.D.s, but there are more and more Ph.D.s teaching these days. In rare cases, a whole department might have Ph.D.s and require publication to be considered for a full-time job and tenure, such as the psychology department here." Some four-year colleges also view the role of their faculty almost exclusively as teachers and do not require PFT. However, it is my impression that the number of such colleges is diminishing as more of them adopt the teacher-scholar model.

Viewing tenure as a game and publishing as a rule of that game (assuming, of course, that it is) could reduce the likelihood of your committing academic suicide. If you accepted a tenure-track position that required publication and realized early in your probationary period that you were not going to meet this expectation in even a minimal way, you would seek another position rather than waiting to be denied tenure and terminated following your up or out year. You would either decide to make a career change or to seek a position at an institution, such as a community college, that does not require PFT.

A department chairperson is supposed to recommend terminating the employment of a junior faculty member who is not making acceptable progress toward tenure before the faculty member's up or out year. However, the chairperson might not do so, particularly if the faculty member is a good teacher or does more than his or her fair share of advising and departmental committee work. Replacing a faculty member requires a considerable investment of time and energy by the department chairperson. Also, recommending termination or nonrenewal of contract is likely to be unpleasant for the chairperson. By keeping the nonpublishing person around, courses will be taught, advising and committee work will be done, and best of all, someone other than the department chairperson will assume the unpleasant responsibility of terminating the employment of the nontenured faculty member.

If you accept a tenure-track position that requires scholarly publication, viewing tenure as a game and publishing as a rule of that game can maximize the likelihood of your satisfying this requirement. There are several reasons. First, it provides a compelling answer to the question of why you should publish if you do not particularly enjoy doing it. Of course, if you strongly dislike scholarly publishing, you probably will not want to accept this type of position.

A second reason why it is advantageous to view scholarly publishing as a game is that doing so can help you to cope with failure. Just as a baseball player does not always get a hit when he or she comes up to bat, a scholar does not always get an acceptance when he or she submits a manuscript to a journal. Sometimes a baseball player fails to get a hit because he or she is playing poorly. Likewise, a scholar might get a rejection because there is something wrong with a manuscript. If a good baseball player is not getting hits because of playing poorly, the player will attempt to determine the problem and correct it. Likewise, a successful scholar who gets a manuscript rejected will attempt to determine what is wrong with the manuscript and revise it. Finally, a good baseball player will not give up but will accept having bad days as part of the game. Likewise, a successful scholar who gets manuscripts rejected will not cease trying to publish. He or she will accept having manuscripts rejected as a part of the game and will revise and resubmit ones that are not fatally flawed.

There is at least one other reason why it would be advantageous for you to view scholarly publishing as a game. By doing so you are likely to regard reviewers and editors as fallible. Like umpires and referees, their judgments can be wrong. In fact, their incorrect judgments can go beyond merely being errors. For example, they can recommend the rejection of a manuscript if one of the conclusions in it casts doubt on the validity of one of their beliefs — particularly one that they have expressed in print. Other reasons why reviewers and editors recommend rejecting a publishable manuscript are described elsewhere in the book. Strategies for minimizing the likelihood of losing in this way — that is, not getting a publishable article accepted for publication      also are described elsewhere in the book.

## REQUIREMENTS FOR WINNING

Before beginning to play any game, your first question is likely to be, What do I have to do to win? You obviously would find it both frustrating and anxiety-arousing to play a game in which you did not know specifically what you had to do to win — that is, one in which the requirements for winning were stated vaguely. Unfortunately, PFT tends to be that kind of game. One of the professors whom I interviewed described the ambiguity in the requirements for tenure at his university rather graphically:

Here administrators go out of their way to try to avoid telling you either verbally or in writing (particularly in writing) the requirements for tenure and/or promotion. The university does have a rather vague policy which states that you have to nearly be God to obtain either, but few specifics. This is always a problem when new faculty ask me what they need to do. I, unfortunately, can only tell them what I expect from them but not what the upper administration can expect. As you might expect, budgetary concerns also seem to have an effect upon the requirements. Perhaps, in the ideal world that should not be the case, but in the real world it is very much the case.

Unfortunately, the requirements for promotion and tenure at most colleges and universities tend to be somewhat vague, particularly with regard to publishing. Such vagueness provides the institution with a defense if sued for denial of promotion or tenure, particularly if the reason that it gave for denying them was a less than adequate publication record. It would be difficult for a person who is denied tenure for this reason to prove that his or her publication record is adequate if the requirements are vague and his or her publication record is not particularly strong.

The best defense against being denied tenure for this reason is having a strong publication record — that is, a publication record that obviously surpasses what a reasonable person would regard as being a minimally adequate one. The reasonable person standard is the one that a court would use to decide if you had been denied tenure unfairly. Few colleges and universities will attempt to deny you tenure on the grounds of inadequate scholarship if they suspect you probably can document that they have awarded tenure to persons with weaker publication records than yours and who had similar teaching and service records.

## THE RULES

The PFT game, like all games, has rules. The following are examples of publishing-related ones:

A participant must have the courage to write.

The general topic of the paper must be of significant interest to the readers of the journal to which it is submitted.

The specific issue(s) with which a paper deals should be of current interest.

The relevance of the specific issue(s) with which a paper deals should be communicated clearly to readers (including referees).

The manuscript style is that specified in the journal's information for authors.

The length of the manuscript is no longer than absolutely necessary and does not exceed the journal's guideline for maximum article length.

The manuscript is written clearly and is free of spelling and grammatical errors.

The manuscript shows both an awareness and understanding of relevant contemporary literature, and the literature review is sharply focused.

The findings reported are related to the existing body of knowledge.

Neither the findings nor conclusions challenge any gut level beliefs of reviewers.

When a manuscript or book proposal is rejected, it is revised and submitted to another journal or book editor, unless, of course, it is fatally flawed.

Although the author grieves when a manuscript or book proposal is rejected, he or she accepts such rejection as being a part of the game and does not become demoralized when it occurs.

The following are examples of tenure-related rules:

Publish an adequate number of papers in refereed journals that your colleagues
   consider to be respectable.

Be the sole author of some of the papers.

For collaborative papers establish beyond a reasonable doubt that you made a
   significant contribution to them.

Publish at least one peer-reviewed paper a year in a respected journal.

Identify a niche within which your research can earn you a national reputation
   and begin to do what is necessary to achieve that reputation.

Seek extramural funding support for your research.

Involve students in your research.

Have at least some publications in an area in which you teach.

Maintain a low profile for publishing projects that produce income.

These rules and their many implications for winning at the PFT game are
discussed elsewhere in the book.

## STRATEGIES FOR WINNING

Just as the PFT game has rules, it also has strategies for applying these
rules that maximize the likelihood of winning. These strategies enable a
publication record to be communicated in a way that is likely to result in it
being considered adequate. That is, they communicate it in a way that will
be likely to elicit a favorable semantic reaction. A semantic reaction,
according to Korzybski (1958, p. 24), is "the psychological reaction of a
given individual to words and language and other symbols and events in
connection with their meanings." Thus, the term semantic reaction refers
to a person's reaction to a stimulus based on the meaning that the stimulus
has for him or her. The meaning can be one of attraction or revulsion. The
former leads to acceptance and the latter, rejection.

The stimulus to which you are seeking a favorable semantic reaction
here consists of the pages in the promotion and tenure document on which
your publication record is communicated. The semantic reactions of a
vice president for academic affairs, one or more deans, and the members
of one or more promotion and tenure committees to these pages will determine whether your publication record will be considered adequate. The
following are strategies that you can use to maximize the likelihood that it
will be considered adequate:

Document your contribution to each collaborative publication so that it is clear
   that you deserved to be listed as a coauthor rather than merely being

acknowledged for your assistance.

Use any textbooks you have authored or coauthored (particularly undergraduate ones) to document teaching effectiveness rather than scholarship.

Communicate unambiguously that you are not basing your bid for tenure on publications you have in newsletters and other nonrefereed media unless you can document that they embody serious scholarship.

Have your publications evaluated by highly respected scholars in your field and include their evaluations and a statement that establishes them as being top scholars in your field.

Document that your program of publication or research is sufficiently highly respected in the academic community for it to be supported by funding (assuming, of course, that you have received some).

Communicate that you did not publish just to receive tenure and that you will continue to be a productive scholar.

Document that your publications have had an impact on scholarship in your field (by numbers of citations, and so forth).

Document that you are becoming nationally (perhaps even internationally) recognized as a scholar.

These and other strategies for influencing semantic reactions to your publication record are discussed in depth elsewhere in the book.

## PUBLICATION AS AN EXCUSE FOR DENYING TENURE

Your publication record can be deemed inadequate for reasons other than it being so. This is particularly likely to happen if your colleagues do not like you or do not regard you as a team player. One of my interviewees, who is a senior professor in a science department, stated: "It sounds a little cynical, but basically, the main criteria for promotion and tenure is to be 'well-liked' by faculty, students, and administration. The policies and procedures are mainly used to justify decisions that are already in the minds of your peers."

Because many academics find it uncomfortable to refuse to support a bid for tenure for personality-related reasons, they will use something else as justification for doing so. A candidate's publication record is a likely choice. The best defense here is having a strong publication record — one that a grievance committee would be likely to regard as adequate for promotion and tenure — and good interpersonal skills.

# 2

# Fear of Writing for Publication

Polls routinely confirm that public speaking is our number-one fear. ... Writing is merely public speaking on paper, but to a much larger audience. For some, writing to publish is even more daunting than speaking in public. Spoken words blow away in the wind. Published ones last as long as the paper on which they're printed.

— Keyes, 1995, p. 8

Writing for publication can produce anxiety and can continue to do so throughout your academic career. That is the bad news. The good news is that you can learn to cope with the anxiety. Hundreds of thousands of academics have done so. We will consider in this chapter why writing for publication tends to cause anxiety and how writers, particularly academic ones, have coped with the anxiety.

It takes courage to write for publication. As one of my interviewees stated: "Of course it takes courage to publish. And it's very anxiety-arousing. In fact, it takes courage to do anything worthwhile, and often the doing of it causes some degree of stress. With encouragement (note that 'courage' is the root word here), most things are possible for someone who is qualified, competent and who has the will to get on." Nevertheless, publishing is not always an act of courage. As another interviewee pointed out: " Some campuses put too much pressure on faculty to publish. It may be more courageous 'not' to do so—that is, to resist the pressure to publish for publication's sake." Although I can certainly respect the integrity of someone without tenure who refuses to publish for publication's sake, I would not be particularly surprised if he or she were denied tenure. The person would not be playing the game according to the rules. To win at most colleges and universities, it is necessary to publish. However, it certainly is desirable that at least some of a scholar's publications make a significant contribution.

## IS ANXIETY ABOUT WRITING FOR PUBLICATION UNDESIRABLE?

It is normal to have some anxiety about writing for publication. The extent to which it interferes with writing for publication is largely a function of how it is viewed. If it is viewed as an impediment to doing so, it is likely to be one. However, if coping with it is viewed as a challenge, anxiety is likely to interfere less with the writing process.

Regarding the anxiety associated with writing for publication as a challenge rather than a peril can do more than merely reduce the extent to which it impedes the process. Such anxiety actually can fuel the process, thereby increasing productivity.

Creative people of all kinds use anxiety as an energy source. . . . Gripping writing results from intensity, and intensity is the flip side of fear. Some writers don't feel that they're getting anywhere until anxiety kicks in.

A tranquil writer can have trouble staying focused on the task at hand. Those who convert fear into focus have a potent weapon in their arsenal. (Keyes, 1995, pp. 127, 130)

Although scholarly writing rarely is characterized as being gripping, the extent to which it is gripping significantly influences its impact. A book or article that does not hold a reader's attention is likely to have less impact than one that does. There are suggestions for increasing the "grippingness" of scholarly writing elsewhere in the book.

One of my primary objectives is to assist you in developing an attitude toward publishing-related anxiety that will facilitate, rather than hinder, your ability to create an adequate publication record for promotion and tenure. Not having such an attitude is one of the main reasons why assistant professors end up publishing too little to be promoted and tenured.

# REASONS WHY WRITING FOR PUBLICATION
# AND TENURE CAN CAUSE ANXIETY

There are a number of reasons why writing for publication and tenure can cause anxiety.

## Risk and Failure

Taking a risk almost always produces anxiety because it creates an opportunity for failing. Writing for publication involves taking risks, thereby creating opportunities for failing. These risks include taking on a writing project and failing to complete it, submitting a manuscript for publication and having it rejected, and having a publication ignored or criticized. Although risking writing for publication can lead to failure, not doing so is almost certain to lead to failure—that is, failure to get tenure, promotion, merit pay increases, grants, and so forth.

## Rejection

Rejection and the fear of it create anxiety. Anyone who writes for publication is likely to experience rejection. Manuscripts and proposals often are rejected. The stated positions and conclusions likewise also can be criticized, ignored, or otherwise rejected.

Rejection or the fear of it, by itself, can be sufficient to keep an assistant professor from creating an adequate publication record for tenure. This is particularly likely to happen if the first manuscript that he or she submits to a journal is rejected. It also can happen if the first manuscript is not accepted as is. The latter scenario caused a colleague of mine who had considerable potential as a scholar to not become one. Of the approximately 150 papers that I have published in professional journals, fewer than a dozen were accepted as is. I have also had dozens of papers rejected by journals. Rejection is as much a part of the publishing for tenure game as is striking out in baseball.

## Being Wrong

The thought of publishing a finding or conclusion that is wrong can cause anxiety. If a scholar is highly productive, it is likely that he or she will occasionally publish findings or conclusions that are wrong or misleading. This reality has been recognized by philosophers of science in the characteristic of the scientific method that they refer to as comprehensiveness or scope of knowledge (Silverman, 1998b). According to this, all findings and conclusions are tentative and subject to change whenever new information becomes available. Consequently, every conclusion should be assumed to be preceded by the following statement: "With the information I currently have available, it is likely that . . . ."

## Not Enough Time for Scholarly Activities

Most assistant professors have a teaching load to which they must devote considerable time. This is particularly true during their first few years of employment because each course they teach is a new preparation. They also are likely to have committee and advising responsibilities. Furthermore, they are likely to have family responsibilities. Consequently, they very often are unlikely to have large blocks of time during the academic year for scholarly activities. The realization that you must publish for tenure and the assumption that you need large blocks of time to do it would tend, not surprisingly, to cause anxiety.

Writing for as little as 30 minutes a day, almost every day, can yield a publishing record that is adequate for tenure. I have written in this manner for 25 years; by so doing, I was able to write (and have published) more than a dozen books and more than 100 journal articles while carrying a full faculty load. This method of writing is described in detail elsewhere in the book.

## Professional Envy and Jealousy

You are particularly likely to encounter professional envy and jealousy — whether anticipated or perceived — if:

you are in a department where few people publish;

as a result of your publications, you receive grants, and are invited to participate in conferences, be on the editorial board of a scholarly journal, or be on a committee of your national association; or

your colleagues believe you are making money from your publications — for example, as the author or coauthor of textbooks.

If you are productive as a scholar, you undoubtedly will encounter professional envy and jealousy from at least a few colleagues. Although you cannot keep envy and jealousy from occurring, there are a few things you can do to minimize their impact on your prospects for promotion and tenure, including:

maintaining a low profile with your colleagues regarding your scholarly activities — not concealing them, but not treating them as being a big deal;

not asking to be excused from advising, committee, and teaching responsibilities because of your scholarly activities; and

maintaining a high profile with your dean, vice president for academic affairs, and possibly your department chairperson with regard to your scholarly activities (the perception that you have upper administrative support will tend to discourage colleagues from attempting to sabotage your bid for promotion and tenure).

## Scholarly Activities Hurt Relationships with Family and Friends

If you have a full teaching load, you are likely to be working, at least occasionally, on writing and publishing projects evenings, weekends, and during vacation periods. These are times when you would otherwise be available to family and friends. Both family and friends are likely to resent, at least a little, that you have less time available for them, which could cause you to feel guilty. As one of my interviewees commented: "Your family can undermine your writing efforts without ever saying anything. And the way they undermine it is by making you feel like you're taking time away from them."

One way that you may be able to reduce the negative impact of your writing and publishing activities on your relationships with family and friends, at least a little, is by working on them for 30 minutes or so almost every day. If you do this, there will be fewer large blocks of time during which you will not be available to family and friends.

## Scholarly Activities Interfere with Teaching or with Teacher-Student Relationships

Assistant professors are expected to teach, and most are motivated to do it well and have good relationships with students. It usually is necessary for them to spend considerable time on activities related to course preparation during the first few years of teaching. Because many beginning assistant professors assume that they need large blocks of time to pursue scholarly activities and do not want their scholarly activities to interfere with their teaching, they neglect these activities during the first few years of their probationary period. Although this strategy enables them to cope successfully with anxiety related to teaching, it tends to work against their developing an adequate publication record for promotion and tenure. The suggestion I have made elsewhere in this chapter to write or otherwise pursue scholarly activities for 30 minutes or so almost every day is unlikely to interfere with course preparations or other teaching-related activities and is likely to yield at least one publishable paper a year.

### Lack of Self-Confidence as an Independent Scholar

If you recently completed your terminal degree or your postdoctoral studies, it is likely that most, if not all, of your writing and publishing has been in collaboration with established scholars. It would not be surprising, therefore, if you were experiencing anxiety because of lack of confidence in your ability to function independently. Although it is normal to experience anxiety for this reason, it is not particularly comfortable to do so. Perhaps the best way to cope with such anxiety is to begin writing and hopefully publishing as soon as possible. If you have already found a niche in your field to explore, begin doing so. If you have not yet identified such a niche, you might begin to write your dissertation or other research you have completed but not yet published. Although publishing such research might not make a huge contribution to scholarship in your field, it should help you develop confidence in your ability to function as an independent scholar. While doing this, you can search for a niche in which you could make a significant contribution to scholarship in your field. Some strategies that you can use to facilitate your search are described in Chapter 3.

### Lack of Self-Confidence as a Writer

Your lack of self-confidence can be more as a writer than as a researcher. You might be confident in your ability to do research but not in your ability to communicate what you learn well enough to have it published. The thought of writing up your research can cause so much anxiety that you do not do it. I have known scholars who have done considerable significant research but have never published, or have published little, for this reason. The bottom line in this case probably is fear of submitting manuscripts to journals and having them rejected.

If you can communicate successfully with students, you probably can write well enough to have your manuscripts accepted for publication by a journal that is academically respectable, even if it is not the most prestigious journal in your field. If you believe that what you have to report can advance scholarship in your field, it really is not necessary that it be published in the most prestigious journal. It is only necessary that it be published in a peer-reviewed journal that is abstracted by the computerized databases in your field.

## Perfectionism

Perfectionism can result in little, or no, scholarly output. If you delay submitting a manuscript to a journal until it is perfect, you might never submit it because it will never reach the point where it is impossible to improve it further. According to Keyes (1995): "A key moment that distinguishes would-be writers from those who publish is the one when fingers open to let an envelope holding a manuscript disappear into the dark abyss of a mailbox" (p. 28). You have to be willing to submit a manuscript when it is reasonably well written     not perfect. Most grammatical and stylistic errors that remain will be corrected by the copyeditor.

## Procrastination

Even the thought of writing for publication tends to cause anxiety. As the well-known novelist John Steinbeck once commented: "I suffer as always from the fear of putting down the first line. It is amazing the terrors, the magics, the prayers, the straightening shyness that assails one." It is normal to put off doing tasks that we expect to make us uncomfortable. Some assistant professors tell themselves and others that their teaching, advising, and other responsibilities do not allow them sufficient time to write for publication, but their real reason for not doing it is to avoid a task that makes them feel uncomfortable. Almost anyone can find 30 minutes a day to write.

## Writer's Block

Anxiety about scholarly writing is normal. How you react to it determines whether it will block or enhance your ability to write. According to Keyes (1995):

Finding the courage to write does not involve erasing or "conquering" ones fears. Working writers aren't those who have eliminated their anxiety. They are the ones who keep scribbling while their heart races and their stomach churns, and who mail manuscripts with trembling fingers. . . . Trying to deny, avoid, numb, or eradicate the fear of writing is neither possible nor desirable. Anxiety is not only an inevitable part of the writing process but a necessary part. . . . A state of anxiety is the writer's natural habitat. (pp. 12–13)

Accepting the presence of anxiety while writing as both normal and desirable can both prevent and eliminate writer's block.

Incidentally, the stronger your fear of and desire to avoid writer's block, the more likely it is to occur. Expecting to be able to write leads to being able to write and expecting to be blocked leads to being blocked. Having a 30 minute or so daily writing schedule can help to create an expectation of being able to write and, thereby, reduce the likelihood of becoming blocked.

How can anxiety facilitate your ability to write? It can help you to concentrate (focus) on the task at hand. "Writers who are afraid of a manuscript but work on it anyway will give that work the same degree of concentration that they'd pay to a forest fire whose heat has begun to sear their skin" (Keyes, 1995, p. 130).

## Not Identifying a Niche for Research and Publication

It can cause anxiety to know that you are expected to become a nationally recognized scholar, particularly if you have not identified a niche within your field. Some strategies that may help you to identify such a niche are described in Chapter 3.

## Not Securing Adequate Funding or Support

The fact that your scholarly publishing might depend on funding (particularly extramural funding) or cooperation from others can produce anxiety. If one is not fully in control, contemplation as well as execution of the project tends to cause anxiety. The kinds of cooperation needed could involve one or more of the following: funding, equipment, subjects, or coauthors

To create an adequate publishing record for promotion and tenure, it is better to need less cooperation from others. The more you have to rely on others to complete a project, the more likely the project is to not be completed. Because the goal of creating an adequate publication record for tenure is likely to be more important to you at the beginning of your academic career than that of making a highly significant contribution to your field, it would probably be wise that at least some of your initial projects not require a great deal of cooperation from others to complete. Although such projects, by themselves, are unlikely to yield a strong national reputation, they are likely to yield an adequate publication record for promotion and tenure.

Many in academia tend to assume that it is desirable for a scholar at the beginning of his or her academic career to coauthor papers with a published mentor. Although such a mentoring experience certainly can assist a beginning scholar in learning his or her craft, it can be risky for at least two reasons. First, the mentor might be so busy with other projects and responsibilities that he or she will not make his or her contribution(s) to a project in a timely fashion. Several of my colleagues have had publications delayed by years for this reason. Second, if most of your publications when you go up for promotion and tenure were coauthored with a mentor, at least some members of your committee could question your ability to function as an independent scholar. They are particularly likely to do so if your mentor was your dissertation advisor.

## No Longer Being Able to View Oneself as "a Giant in Chains"

Risk can make you anxious and cause you to experience failure. A person can attempt to minimize the likelihood of experiencing failure under a particular set of circumstances by viewing himself or herself as a giant in chains under that set of circumstances. An assistant professor, for example, might believe that he or she would make a substantial scholarly contribution if his or her faculty load were small enough to allow time for research. The chains here would be teaching, advising, and committee responsibilities. Although viewing yourself in this way could keep you from experiencing failure in the short term, doing so is unlikely to yield an adequate publication record for promotion and tenure and, consequently, is likely to cause you to experience failure in the long term.

## Completing a Project and Having to Find Another

After completing a project, you are likely to experience a moment of satisfaction followed by anxiety. Although completion of a project is certainly desirable, it can cause a loss for which you are likely to grieve, thereby producing at least a little depression and anxiety. As one interviewee commented: "Expect the post-partum depression syndrome when you send off a manuscript. The first time I had it, I didn't know what it was. I was just lower than a snake's belly." The cure is to begin another project. You easily can become addicted to scholarly publishing in this way. I have been addicted to scholarly publishing for more than 25 years. However, I regard it as being a positive addiction (Glasser, 1976) — one from which the benefits far outweigh the losses.

## COPING STRATEGIES

Several strategies can help you cope with the fear of writing for publication.

### Write Daily

Maintaining a relatively short, daily writing schedule is one of the main strategies that many authors (including myself) use to cope with writing-related anxiety and writer's block. Once you get into the habit of beginning to write at a particular time each day, you find that sentences and paragraphs begin to flow almost immediately. Because nothing succeeds like success or fails like failure, this flow tends to make writing for publication less fearful. Factors to consider when establishing a daily writing schedule are discussed elsewhere in the book.

### Compose First, Worry Later

If you feel a strong need to get every sentence and paragraph perfect before moving on, you are likely to feel anxious about the act of writing and, consequently, you will probably write very little. Most successful authors view the act of writing as a two-stage process. The first is composing — that is, getting the material on paper or in a computer's memory. The second is editing the material to eliminate grammatical, spelling, and stylistic errors and to improve its clarity and organization. Word processing software can be particularly helpful during the second of these stages.

### Accept Your Need for Rituals and Totems

Many, perhaps most, authors use rituals and totems when writing that both reduce their anxiety and create an expectation of not being blocked. Most such rituals are likely to seem irrational to others. For example, "Early in his career, John Cheever [the novelist] put on a business suit, then went from his apartment to a room in the basement where he hung his suit on a hanger and wrote in his underwear" (Keyes, 1995, p. 141). Authors' totems include the devices they use for writing. James Michner, for example, throughout his career drafted chapters on 1950s-vintage office model manual typewriters because he believed that doing so somehow facilitated his ability to write. His belief in this was so strong that he insisted on having such a typewriter available to him whenever he was writing away from his home or office. My rituals include beginning to write as close as possible to 7:00 a.m., and my totems include being surrounded while writing by a collection of more than 100 antique cameras.

Because it is normal for authors to use rituals and totems to keep from becoming blocked, you should not feel guilty about relying on them, even if they would seem irrational to others. As long as your rituals and totems do no harm to yourself or others, they can be useful devices for coping with writing-related anxiety.

## Provide Opportunities for Experiencing a Feeling of Accomplishment

A writing project, particularly a book, can take a great deal of time to complete. Although you undoubtedly will experience at least a momentary feeling of accomplishment when you complete it, you also should experience feelings of accomplishment along the way. If you do not, you are unlikely to be able to keep yourself sufficiently motivated to complete the project.

There are several strategies that can enable you to experience such feelings of accomplishment, including the following:

Establish a daily, easily achievable word quota. If you set the quota low enough, you can get feelings of accomplishment from frequently being ahead of schedule.

Regard a publishing project as being multiple task rather than single task. Drafting a section or chapter, for example, would be a task. Completing each could bring a feeling of accomplishment. Incidentally, you might find it reinforcing to diagram the tasks needed to complete a project using project planning software, mount the printout on your office wall, and cross out (with a marker) the box that represents each task after it is completed.

## Talk with Persons Who Are Good Listeners and Who Are Not Threatened by Your Projects

Talking about what you are writing with persons who are both good listeners and supportive can be helpful. It can be particularly helpful if doing so reinforces your feeling that you have the ability to communicate effectively and what you are trying to communicate is worthwhile. In contrast, talking about a project with someone who is neither supportive nor a good listener can be sufficiently upsetting to reduce the likelihood of your completing it. If you are uncertain about how supportive a listener would be, it would perhaps be best not to discuss it with him or her, unless, of course, you wanted someone to serve as devil's disciple.

### Working on Several Journal Articles or Book Projects at the Same Time

It is not unusual while working on a project to be temporarily unable to proceed. There can be a number of reasons, including equipment or subjects being unavailable. You are less likely to experience anxiety when this happens if you have another project to work on while you are waiting.

### Avoid Projects You Might Not Be Able to Complete

Your primary scholarly goal during your probationary period should be to create an adequate publication record for promotion and tenure. Having this goal, there are several types of scholarly projects you would be wise to avoid because you might not be able to complete them by the time you are considered for promotion and tenure. These include the following:

longitudinal studies, particularly ones for which preliminary data are unlikely to be publishable;

studies that require subjects, equipment, or funding you are not almost certain to have available; or

studies that will take so much time to complete that you will not have sufficient time to complete the other publishing projects you need to create an adequate publication record

### Avoid Projects That Are Unlikely to be Publishable

Some projects are more likely to be publishable than others. Types of projects that are less likely than others to be publishable include:

studies that are only likely to be publishable if they turn out a certain way (for example, if there is a statistically significant difference);

books for which the author does not have a publishing contract;

books that are unlikely to attract a publisher because the potential market for them is too small; or

articles and books on a topic that would be appropriate for only a few journals or
  book publishers

Although some such projects have the potential to make a very significant
contribution to a field, they are very risky to undertake during the probationary period.

## Incorporate a Jenga Philosophy

Jenga is a strategy game in which you build a tower with small, brick-
like wood blocks. The object of the game is to remove a block from the
tower and place it on top of the tower without causing the tower to fall. A
player scans the blocks in the tower for the one that when removed is least
likely to cause the tower to fall. The player does not know which block
will be the loosest before his or her turn. A successful player examines all
possibilities before committing to removing a particular block. The strat
egy for winning at this game is to be constantly open to exploiting opportunities that arise.

Similarly, the strategy for winning at the publishing for tenure game is
to be constantly open to exploiting opportunities that arise. Opportunities
to become involved with projects that are likely to yield publications can
arise unexpectedly. For example, if you are in a healthcare-related field,
you might have an opportunity to do a case study on a patient who has an
unusual condition. Such a project might not be related to your current
research. Because your main goal during your probationary period should
be to create an adequate publication record for promotion and tenure, you
should exploit such opportunities to help you achieve it. Doing so also can
lead you to a research area that you might find more interesting and fruit-
ful than the one you are pursuing currently.

## Getting into the "Zone"

Runners talk about the experience of being in the zone. This is a very
pleasant trance-like state. It is probably because of "natural opiates such
as endorphins that flood our bodies when we're under stress. Such opiates
induce a euphoric state of intense concentration" (Keyes, 1995, p. 190).
Consequently, being in the zone is having a legal drug-induced high that is
both free and safe.

Many authors write while in the zone (see Keyes, 1995). Writing —
particularly at a set time each day — can induce it. While in the zone,
authors experience a reduction in writing-related anxiety and an increase

in the ability to concentrate. Words, sentences, and paragraphs flow easily. Time passes quickly. Writing is enjoyable. One of the benefits of beginning to write at about the same time each day is that doing so is likely to get you into the zone. This is particularly likely to happen if the time of day you write is one when you tend to be alert. That is, if you are a morning person, your time to write should be in the morning. If you are an evening person, your time to write should be in the evening.

# 3

# Selecting a Project

Perhaps the best way to find a topic to write about is to stay abreast of your professional surroundings. Writers read extensively. They keep up with journals in their field as well as allied fields. They attend conferences. They get onto a computer bulletin board in their field and share ideas and essays with others. . . . They dialogue with students. . . . In short, they are in touch with their environment.
— Cantor, 1993, p. 18

You begin the publishing for tenure (PFT) game by selecting a project. The project you select is most likely to be an article in a printed journal, an article in an electronic journal, a printed book, or a book that is published in electronic form (for example, on a CD-ROM disk). However, it could be something else. For example, a colleague of mine, a number of years ago, published an oral history of jazz on audiotape that he had peer reviewed and used successfully to support his bid for promotion and tenure. The critical thing is that the project is peer reviewed either before or after publication, preferably the former.

## REQUIREMENTS

To win at the PFT game, you must be able to convince your institution's promotion and tenure committee and others that you are a competent, productive scholar and are likely to continue being productive if granted tenure. To do this, you must select projects that satisfy several requirements.

### Be Publishable in Peer-Reviewed Media

It is critical that the publications you submit for promotion and tenure are peer reviewed. Although they can be peer reviewed either before or after publication, the former is preferable.

When selecting projects, the number of existing outlets for publishing them that are peer reviewed should be taken into consideration. A paper, for example, that would be of interest to the readership of a large number of journals would be more likely to get published than one that would be of interest to the readership of only a few journals. The peer review process is a highly subjective one, and a publishable paper easily can get rejected by one or more journals. Also, the reviewers' comments that accompany a rejection letter can be used to improve a paper. Consequently, the more journals for which a paper is appropriate, the more likely it is to eventually be positively peer reviewed and published.

Including publications that were not peer reviewed in your application for promotion and tenure can do you more harm than good. Examples would be articles published in newsletters or on the Internet and self-published and vanity press books. The only way that such publications are certain to evoke a positive response by the members of a promotion and tenure committee is if they suggest that you are developing a national reputation as a scholar in your field. An example of such a publication would be an invited review of a scholarly book in your field. You would be wise to list non–peer-reviewed publications in a separate section with a note indicating they were included to serve as documentation that you are beginning to develop a national reputation.

### Be Relatively Free of Controversy

The more controversial the content of a project, the less likely it will be reviewed positively and get published. Also, the more controversial the content of a project, the less likely all of the members of a promotion and tenure committee will evaluate it positively. You would be unwise to undertake research, for example, that is intended to question a widely accepted theory in your field during the probationary period. The less controversial the topics and the possible outcomes of projects you undertake during the probationary period, the better.

It might not be possible to avoid controversy. You can minimize the risk of a negative reaction from reviewers by presenting all sides of controversial topics and outcomes without bias.

### Still Be of Interest When You Are Considered for Promotion and Tenure

It is risky to have publications that no longer might be of interest to scholars when you are considered for promotion and tenure. Studies of this type include attempts to test theories in which interest might be fleeting. If most of your publications deal with topics that are no longer of interest, a promotion and tenure committee member could raise the question of whether you are likely to continue to be a productive scholar or will be respected nationally as one.

### Be Easy to Document Your Contributions to Coauthored Publications

Your publication record should communicate to the members of your institution's promotion and tenure committee and others that you are capable of functioning as an independent scholar. If you are a coauthor or not the first author on almost all of your publications one or more committee members could question your ability to function independently. It is important that you be able to document that your contribution to the publication was more than what one would expect from a research assistant. Such a concern particularly is likely if most of your coauthored publications are with your dissertation advisor.

### Yield at Least One Publication Each Year

One question that is asked almost always during promotion and tenure deliberations concerns the candidate's commitment to scholarship. Publishing regularly during the probationary period is likely to be interpreted as having such a commitment, whereas publishing only toward the end of the period is likely to be interpreted solely as an attempt to meet a tenure requirement. If most of your publications are at the end of your probationary period and the reason for this is likely to suggest to the committee that you do have a commitment to scholarship, you would be wise to include a statement in your application giving the reason.

### Identify Your Niche

Developing a national or international reputation in a field requires becoming widely recognized as an authority on a topic, or niche, within that field. It is desirable for the focus for your research and publication activities to be such a niche, at least during the latter portion of your probationary period. This focus indicates that you are a true scholar—not just someone who is trying merely to meet a requirement for tenure. Then too, it maximizes the likelihood that you will be invited to participate in conferences, write chapters for books, review papers for journals, or serve on committees of your national professional association during your probationary period. You can use such invitations as evidence that scholars in your field respect your research and publications and, consequently, you have at least laid a foundation for developing a national or international reputation.

### Allow You to Involve Students

One of the responsibilities of an assistant professor—often the main one—is teaching. A component of this responsibility is training students to not only be consumers of knowledge, but producers of it as well. One way to do this is to provide opportunities for students to participate in your scholarly activities. Their participation could be limited to assisting you in gathering or analyzing data, or it also could include doing a project (for example, a master's thesis) that is a component of your research program. University promotion and tenure committees tend to react favorably to candidates who use their research activities for both teaching and scholarship.

### Attract Extramural Funding

Even if securing extramural funding for your scholarly activities is not a requirement for promotion and tenure in your department, doing so is likely to enhance your prospects for being promoted and tenured. If it is a requirement, it is crucial that you choose a project that is likely to be fundable, even if it is not one you are highly motivated to do. You are playing a game, and to maximize the odds of winning at it (that is, getting tenure), you must follow the rules. It is possible, incidentally, that once you begin the project you will become highly motivated to do it.

## IDENTIFICATION STRATEGIES

Now that we have considered the requirements for an ideal PFT project, we will examine some strategies that scholars have used to identify possible projects.

### Keeping Up with Journals in Their Field

Research is cumulative, that is, it tends to build on what was published previously. The discussion sections of some articles suggest directions for future research. Furthermore, most studies need to be replicated, particularly if the samples used were not truly random ones.

In addition to direct replications of research projects, systematic replications of them may offer opportunities for publication. Systematic replications are ones in which a single variable is changed. Consequently, they provide information about the generality of findings. If, for example, a research study were conducted using children from a suburban school, repeating the study with children from an inner city school would be a systematic replication of the study.

An examination of the most recent copies of a journal also can provide an overview of topics and manuscript styles that the journal editors and editorial board consider publishable. In this regard, one of the authors whom I interviewed suggested the following: "Read backwards the latest issues of journals in your field—that is, beginning with the last page. This facilitates overviewing—rather than detailed reading—and gives you a gestalt regarding what is being published, what is not, and what ought to be. In addition, these overviews will give you some idea of a specific journal's publication format for style, length, and documentation."

### Attending Professional Meetings in Their Field

One tactic for generating research ideas is attending sessions and having informal conversations at professional meetings. Others might suggest good research ideas they do not intend to pursue. Furthermore, studies may be presented that were intended to answer important questions but were poorly designed. You might be able to think of a more valid or reliable methodology for answering one or more of these questions. Finally, you might become aware of research grant opportunities through the grapevine.

### Keeping Up with Journals and Books in Allied Fields

Topics and methodologies in publications from fields even loosely allied to yours can suggest publishable projects for your field. Many of my ideas for publications came from this source. For example, when books began to appear in the mid-1980s about computer applications in medicine and several other healthcare fields, it occurred to me that there should be a market for such a book in the field of speech-language pathology and audiology. I got a contract to write one from Prentice-Hall. Also, a study in a psychology journal on attitudes toward persons in wheelchairs motivated me to do a series of studies on attitudes toward persons with various speech and hearing disorders, utilizing the methodology from the wheelchair study.

### Dialoguing with Colleagues and Students

Many of my ideas for books and articles have been triggered by comments made by colleagues and students. Such comments have come from conversations, e-mail messages, brainstorming sessions, and remarks made by students in class that have as their focus ideas for research and publication projects.

You might find it worthwhile to begin a research and publication idea notebook or an equivalent file on your computer. You can also use an electronic organizer for this purpose (assuming you carry one with you). Good research and publication ideas tend to be forgotten if they are not jotted down.

### Dialoguing with Grant Administrators and Responding to Requests for Proposals

Government agencies and private foundations that offer grants to scholars in your field are likely to have priorities with regard to funding. Administrators from some of them might attend your professional association's national conventions. By informally talking with these administrators about their priorities, you might get an idea for a project that is not only publishable but also fundable. Receiving extramural funding is a requirement for tenure in some departments.

Another grant-related source of research and publication ideas is requests for proposals. An agency, usually a government one, describes a project it is willing to fund and requests proposals for doing it. Most such projects are interdisciplinary and, consequently, require more than one person to do them. If someone at your institution is planning to submit a proposal for such a project, perhaps you can assume responsibility for a piece of it—one that is likely to yield publications. You, however, might decide to avoid projects of this type in which you are prohibited from publishing your findings independently of the rest of the project. A report on the entire project might not be published before you go up for promotion and tenure.

### Dialoguing with Persons Who Have Grants and Might Be Willing to Take on a Collaborator

A person in your field or a related one (at your institution or elsewhere) who has a research grant might be interested in taking on a collaborator for an aspect of the project that is likely to be publishable independently of the rest of it. He or she would most likely be a coauthor of the publication(s) yielded by the collaboration. It is important that, if you coauthor publications before receiving tenure, you are able to document that your contribution was substantial—that is, greater than that of a graduate assistant. Otherwise, the members of your promotion and tenure committee might not regard your coauthored publications as evidence that you are capable of functioning independently as a scholar. It is especially important to provide such documentation if almost all of your publications are coauthored.

### Sending Query Letters to Journal Editors

One of the authors whom I interviewed suggested sending query letters to the editors of one or more of the journals in your field inquiring whether there are any specific topics within your area of expertise for which they are seeking review, tutorial, or other types of papers. You even might want to suggest a topic for a review or tutorial paper and inquire whether the editor would give it serious consideration if submitted.

### Becoming a Coauthor of a Successful Text or Professional Book

If there is a book in your field that has been in print for a long time and the author or a coauthor is close to retiring, he or she might be interested in finding someone to help prepare a new edition and possibly assume responsibility for future editions. The person would probably share royalties with you. Becoming a coauthor of such a book is likely to help you establish a national reputation in your field.

### Identifying Questions That Have Been Asked, but Only Partially Answered

Such questions could be suggested by comments made in journal articles, books, or convention presentations, or by those of colleagues or students. They include questions asked in studies that used small or nonrandom samples. Without replication, the generality of the findings of such studies is uncertain.

### Identifying Questions That Have Not Been Asked, but Should Be

Such questions could arise from a number of sources. One source that exists in all fields is "facts" for which there is a lack of empirical evidence. They are passed on from one generation of scholars to another and rarely, if ever, questioned. They are accepted as facts because the persons who disseminate them are regarded as authorities. One way to identify such questions is to ask yourself what you and others in your field accept as facts and what evidence exists for them.

# 4

# Publishing Options

There is little disagreement among administrators that the most important activity of a faculty member is writing a scholarly book. Faculty in undergraduate (baccalaureate) degree granting colleges may receive more credit than their university colleagues for activities such as reviewing for national journals, authoring newsletters, and writing book reviews. Publication of refereed journal articles likewise will be a primary and important consideration. Articles in national magazines or non-refereed journals rank below traditional research in importance to promotion and tenure.

— Cantor, 1993, p. 8

To win at the publishing for tenure (PFT) game you must publish. There are many options for scholarly publication. In this chapter we will examine some of them.

## PUBLISHING AND COPYRIGHT

Before examining publishing options, we will consider briefly what constitutes publishing, including the ownership of published works. Publishing a work is making copies of it available to others. The number of copies of a work that are published can be as few as one or as many as millions. The work can be a manuscript, audiotape, videotape, drawing, photograph, computer program, or CD-ROM disk.

Any work that you create belongs to you. It is your intellectual property. You own the copyright to it regardless of whether you have registered it with the Copyright Office in the Library of Congress. The framers of the Constitution felt so strongly about authors having the exclusive right to benefit financially and otherwise from their writings and other works of authorship that they gave Congress the following power in Article 1, Section 8: "Congress shall have the power . . . to promote the progress of science and useful arts, by securing for a limited time to authors . . . the *exclusive right* to their . . . writings" (italics added). The mechanism created by Congress for protecting the rights of authors was the copyright. According to the current copyright law (The Copyright Act of 1976), you or your heirs have the exclusive right to profit from your writings and other works until 50 years after your death. You or they can either publish them or assign the right to do so to a publisher.

The right that you give a publisher to publish all or part of a work you have written can be either exclusive or nonexclusive. If it is to be exclusive, you will probably be required to transfer the copyright to the publisher. Strictly speaking, once you transfer the copyright, you can no longer make and distribute copies of the work without the publisher's permission. You no longer own it; the publisher does.

In contrast, if the right that you give a publisher to publish all or part of your work is nonexclusive, you retain the copyright and, consequently, can control both what is published and the manner in which it is published. If, for example, you own the copyright to a journal article and a publisher wishes to include it in an anthology or a professor wishes to include it in a course package, you have the legal right to give or withhold permission to include it. If you decide to give permission to reprint the article and the publisher or college bookstore pays a fee, you will receive the fee. If, however, you give the journal the exclusive right to publish the article (that is, you transferred the copyright to the article to the journal), its editor has the legal right to decide whether to give permission to reprint it. Any permission fees received by the journal for reprinting the article (in whole or part) are unlikely to be shared with you. One option is to offer the journal first North American (or International) serial rights rather than a transfer of copyright. This will enable you to control reprinting of the article. Unfortunately, some journals will not accept an article for publication unless its copyright is transferred to the journal.

Traditionally in academic book publishing, authors do not self-publish. They transfer the copyrights to their books to a publisher who pays them a royalty on each copy sold. This is usually a percentage of the money received by the publisher, rather than of the retail price of the book.

Publishing contracts for academic books are dealt with elsewhere in the book.

As I have indicated previously, it is traditional in journal publishing for authors to transfer copyrights to journals. Journals pay authors no royalty on income they receive from their articles, including permission fees paid by other publishers for reprinting them in anthologies or college bookstores for including them in course packages. To add insult to injury, the author can be assessed a page charge. The page charge, however, may be voluntary rather than mandatory. Failure to pay a voluntary page charge usually will not affect the publication of an article.

Copyright law protects audiotapes, videotapes, drawings, photographs, computer software, and multimedia presentations on CD-ROM disks — like articles and books. If they are not self-published, the copyrights to them usually are transferred to the publisher, and the author is paid a royalty. Publishing contracts for these types of projects are similar to those for academic books.

My main focus in the remainder of this chapter is on types of publications that can be used to document scholarship for promotion and tenure. Undoubtedly, there are others that also can be used for this purpose.

## SCHOLARLY ARTICLES

These are the most common types of publications used for documenting that a junior faculty member is capable of functioning as a scholar. Scholarly articles can range in length from a single page to more than 100 pages, and might report original research or integrate existing literature. They also might be published independently as monographs if they are very long. Some aspects of how articles are written (for example, their reference style) are likely to be specified by the publication in which they appear. The peer review process to which they are subjected before acceptance for publication can range from none to extremely rigorous.

Several options for publishing scholarly articles are described in this section. Some are available in all fields (for example, printed journals) and others (for example, electronic journals) in only certain ones. There, of course, could be publishing options for such articles in your field other than those mentioned here.

### Printed Journals

Printed journals exist in all fields and in almost all languages. Some are published by professional, scientific, or scholarly associations and others by commercial publishers. Some accept almost all manuscripts submitted to them; others accept only a small percentage. Some publish papers on a wide range of topics, and others have a fairly narrow focus. Some have hundreds of subscribers and others have tens of thousands. The subscribers to some are mostly from a single state and those to others are from all states or a number of countries. They may be published weekly, biweekly, monthly, bimonthly, semiannually, or annually. Some publish fewer than 100 pages a year, and some publish thousands of pages a year.

Before selecting a journal to which to submit a manuscript, you should consider several things. First consider to whom the information in the manuscript would be most helpful. It might be those who live in a particular state or anywhere in the country or the world. They might be researchers, practitioners, or students. They might be in a single field or in a number of fields.

You also should consider the prominence of each of the journals to which you might submit the article. If there is more than one journal for which a manuscript would be appropriate, consider which is the most prestigious. Everything else being equal, it is more desirable to publish in journals that are generally regarded as being prestigious. Be aware, however, that highly prestigious journals tend to have large numbers of submissions and, consequently, have higher rejection rates. You initially might want to submit your manuscripts to the most prestigious journals for which they are appropriate. If an article is rejected, you could then revise it, incorporating the comments of the reviewers, and then submit it to less prestigious journals. This strategy is likely to enable you to publish at least some of your papers in relatively high-prestige journals. The only real disadvantage to using it is that it could take longer to have manuscripts accepted for publication than it would if they were submitted initially to relatively low-prestige journals.

The decision whether a manuscript contributes sufficiently to warrant publication is a highly subjective one. Consequently, a manuscript could be rejected by one journal and accepted by another. It is even possible that a relatively high-prestige journal will accept it and a relatively low-prestige one will reject it. If a manuscript is rejected by a journal because its reviewers did not believe that it contributed sufficiently to warrant publication and you do not accept their evaluation, submit it to another journal. If that journal also rejects it for the same reason, submit it to one or more additional journals. A manuscript that makes even a modest contribution will eventually find a home if you do not give up the search. It is particularly worthwhile to try to place every manuscript if tenure decisions regarding the adequacy of publication records at your institution are based almost exclusively on numbers of publications.

## Electronic Journals

Electronic journals are published on the Internet and are a relatively recent phenomenon. There were more than 500 when this chapter was written. Although some of these journals subjected papers to a peer-review process comparable to that for print journals, others did not do so. Consequently, the presumption of an adequate peer-review process that exists for most print journals does not exist for most electronic ones.

One advantage electronic journals might have over print journals is that they might offer a shorter time delay between manuscript acceptance and publication. For print journals, it is not unusual for publication to take a year or longer. Because electronic journals can allow research to be communicated more rapidly, they might be particularly desirable in fields (such as computer-related ones) that are changing rapidly.

Another possible advantage electronic journals have over print journals is accessibility. Articles published in electronic journals can be read on any computer that is linked to the Internet.

Unfortunately, publications in electronic journals do not tend to be as highly respected by persons making tenure decisions as those in print journals. One reason is that they have not been around long enough to be regarded as a traditional medium for scholarly publication. The new kid on the block is always suspect. Another concern is the quality of the peer-review process to which manuscripts are subjected before being accepted for publication. The assumption that articles have been subjected to an adequate peer-review process before publication is more likely to be made for ones published in print journals than for those published in electronic journals. Consequently, if some of the publications listed in your tenure application were in electronic journals, you would be wise to include documentation that they had been adequately peer reviewed before being published.

Until publication in electronic journals is accepted more widely as academically respectable, you would be wise to do most of your pretenure publishing in print journals.

## Chapters in Edited Volumes

These can be very helpful for winning at the PFT game, particularly if the editors are respected widely as scholars and their publishers are academically respectable (for example, university presses). An invitation to contribute a chapter (or chapters) to such a volume is likely to be regarded by the members of your institution's promotion and tenure committee as evidence that you have begun to establish a national reputation in your field.

In return for contributing a chapter (or chapters) to an edited volume, you will probably receive a complimentary copy. You also might receive an honorarium or a royalty, particularly for books that are regarded as being money-makers (for example, textbooks).

## Conference Proceedings

Some conference proceedings only contain abstracts of papers that were presented at a conference, whereas others contain some or all of the papers that were presented. The papers published in such a volume might not have been peer reviewed before publication.

Having an abstract published in a conference proceeding is unlikely to be helpful in supporting a bid for tenure other than serving as documentation for your having presented a paper. Having a paper published in one is unlikely to be particularly helpful either, unless you can document that it was subjected to a rigorous peer-review process before publication.

## Unpublished Convention and Conference Papers

Almost all scholars present papers at professional meetings and distribute copies to interested persons, either in the form of printed copies or by posting the paper on a World Wide Web site. Either way, they are self-publishing the paper. Some credit toward promotion and tenure is likely to be given for such publications. However, it probably will be considerably less than if the paper had been published in a journal because it was not peer reviewed. Consequently, you probably would find it advantageous to rewrite convention and conference papers in a form suitable for journal publication after you have presented them. While doing so, you might be able to improve the papers by taking into consideration criticisms and suggestions from persons who heard the papers presented or read the self-published versions of them.

## Nonacademic Publications

Articles in magazines and newspapers intended for the general public ordinarily are not viewed as scholarly and, consequently, not only are they given little weight by promotion and tenure committees, they can, in fact, have a negative impact on tenure decisions, particularly if they are perceived as having been money-makers.

## OTHER PUBLICATIONS IN JOURNALS AND NEWSLETTERS

There are several other types of publications that you might be able to use to support a bid for promotion and tenure. These are book reviews, letters to the editor, and articles and columns in academic newsletters.

### Book Reviews

Book reviews are published in many professional and scholarly journals. Because a journal's book review editor usually commissions them, persons invited to do the reviews are likely to be assumed by promotion and tenure committees to have at least begun to establish a national reputation in the field with which the books deal. Consequently, if you have been invited to do such reviewing, you can use the reviews as evidence that you have begun to establish such a reputation in your field. Be aware, however, that book reviews are unlikely to be accepted by promotion and tenure committees as substitutes for journal articles. They are particularly unlikely to be accepted as substitutes for journal articles at universities that regard themselves as being research institutions.

### Letters to the Editor

These can be helpful for documenting your ability to function constructively as a scholar. I emphasize the word "constructively" because letters to the editor that are nasty in tone or content are unlikely to enhance your reputation. You can question the methodology or conclusions in an article without appearing to be attacking its author(s). Although your peers might enjoy reading a letter to the editor in which you tear somebody's paper apart in a nasty way, they are highly unlikely to respect you for doing so.

There is another reason why you should make your letters to the editor constructive. Journal editors are constantly seeking reviewers who can objectively evaluate manuscripts without being unnecessarily cruel. If your letters to the editor convey that you have the ability to do this, you might be invited to review manuscripts for that journal. Such an invitation is likely to be regarded by your promotion and tenure committee as evidence that you have begun to develop a national reputation as a scholar.

Of course, if the reviews you write are nasty rather than constructive, your tenure as a reviewer is likely to be short.

### Articles and Columns in Academic Newsletters

Newsletters exist in almost every field. The articles and columns that appear in them are rarely, if ever, peer reviewed. The editor usually makes publication decisions. Because such publications are not peer reviewed, they are unlikely to be accepted by promotion and tenure committees as being equivalent to journal publications. However, you might be able to use them as evidence that you are functioning actively as a scholar in your field or that you have begun to develop a national reputation in it.

## BOOKS

Some books are likely to be helpful for winning at the PFT game and others are not. The determining factor is whether they are likely to be regarded as scholarly. The decision whether a book is scholarly can be very subjective and can be influenced by several factors including its content, its publisher, and the review process to which it was subjected. Generally speaking, the more rigorous the review process the more scholarly the book is thought to be. How content and publisher affect whether a book is viewed as scholarly is discussed elsewhere in this section.

For academic books that you do not intend to self-publish, you would seek a publishing contract. Such contracts are usually awarded from a proposal and a sample chapter or two. It is usually not advisable to complete a book manuscript before seeking a publisher. For practical information about preparing and submitting proposals for academic books, see Silverman (1998a).

There are a number of types of book publishers used by academics. Some of the pros and cons of each for PFT are indicated below.

### University Presses

University presses are probably the safest book publishers for you to use because they are the most likely to be regarded by the members of your promotion and tenure committee as academically respectable. They almost never publish material that could not be regarded as scholarly, and they almost always subject manuscripts to a rigorous peer-review process before acceptance. Furthermore, because it is well known that their books rarely produce much income for authors, books published by them tend to be the least likely to trigger professional envy and jealousy.

University presses can differ in several ways. One way is prestige. Those at Ivy League and Big Ten universities, for example, generally are regarded as being at the upper end of the prestige continuum. However, lesser-known university presses have achieved eminence in a specific field. Marquette University Press, for example, has done so in the field of Roman Catholic theology.

A second way that university presses differ is how they market books. All publish catalogues, list their books in *Books in Print*, and attempt to have their books reviewed in relevant journals. In addition, some exhibit at professional and academic association meetings, promote their books on the World Wide Web and, by mailings, sell books wholesale to trade bookstores, and actively pursue translation, book club, and other rights sales. The latter tend to be ones that have a mandate from their universities to at least pay their own way.

A third way that university presses differ is with respect to the fields in which they publish. Some publish books in many fields and others in only one or two. You, of course, would only submit proposals to ones that publish in your field.

A fourth way that university presses differ is the extent to which author subventions are mandatory. Author subventions are money paid by the author to partially subsidize the cost of publication. Consequently, author subventions for books are similar to page charges for journal articles. Like page charges, they may be voluntary or mandatory. Some university presses only require an author subvention if grant funds are available.

For further information about publishing in university presses, see Parsons (1989).

### Academic Book Publishers

The publisher of this book specializes in academic books. Academic book publishers publish the same types of books as university presses. The main difference is that they are commercial entities. Because they are businesses, the size of the market for a book is likely to be a more important consideration when making publishing decisions than it is for university presses. Proposals might be peer reviewed before being acted on by an editorial board. Like university presses, they vary with regard to prestige, the number of fields in which they publish, and the quality of the marketing they provide. Also like university presses, the books they publish rarely earn very much income for their authors.

Some academic book publishers also publish academic journals. The differences between the journals they publish and those published by professional and academic associations are essentially the same as the differences between the academic books they publish and those published by university presses.

The differences between the functions of academic book publishers and university presses appear to be narrowing. The main reason is that increasingly university administrators are expecting their presses to at least pay their own way and, if possible, be profitable (Parsons, 1989).

Some publishers that advertise as being academic book publishers are really vanity publishers. They will publish almost anything and require an author to subsidize the publication of his or her book. Having a book published by such a publisher is expensive and can actually hurt your chances for promotion and tenure. Vanity book publishers are dealt with further elsewhere in this chapter.

### Professional Book Publishers

These companies publish books for academics and other working professionals. Some of the books they publish are used as textbooks in upper-division undergraduate and graduate classes. Because most professional book publishers have been acquired by large multinational corporate entities, they have become very bottom line oriented. Consequently, they are unlikely to publish a book for which the acquisitions editor (the person to whom proposals are submitted) cannot argue cogently that they are likely to make a profit. It is critical, therefore, to carefully document in the proposal the existence of a market niche for the book you are proposing. It is not safe to assume that the acquisitions editor will be aware of it.

Most professional book publishers have both proposals for professional books and completed manuscripts reviewed. The primary focus of the reviews is more likely to be the market for the book than the quality of its content. However, if reviewers feel that the quality is poor, they will probably indicate that the market for the book will probably be small.

Books published by professional book publishers are not quite as safe to use to support a bid for tenure as ones that are published by university presses and academic book publishers. They might be regarded as not being scholarly or having been inadequately peer reviewed. Furthermore, they may be assumed to have generated considerable income for their author(s), which could trigger professional envy or jealousy.

In contrast, a book published by a professional book publisher can enhance both your reputation in your field and your income more than those published by university presses and academic book publishers. The books they publish are likely to have a larger readership than those published by university presses and academic book publishers because they are actively marketed to working professionals as well as academics. Consequently, their books are likely to yield more income for their author(s).

It is probably safe to have a professional book or two as a part of the publication package for tenure. It is not safe, however, for such books to be the main part of the publication package, particularly if it is not easy to document that they are scholarly. It is safest to have the main part of the publication package be scholarly articles in peer-reviewed journals.

For further information about professional book proposals and publishers, see Silverman (1998a).

## College Textbook Publishers

These publishers have as their primary focus college textbooks, particularly those for high enrollment undergraduate courses. Most also market at least some of their textbooks for upper-division undergraduate and graduate courses to working professionals. However, because working professionals are not their primary focus, they usually do not market books to them as well as do professional book publishers.

It is probably not safe to use college textbooks — particularly those for lower-division undergraduate courses — as evidence of scholarship for promotion and tenure unless you are at a college that has a history of accepting them as such. A college at which it is safe to use them for meeting the publishing requirement for tenure is more likely to be a two-year rather than a four-year one and one that places more emphasis on undergraduate teaching than on research. You should be able to get information from your dean or your vice president for academic affairs about the probable impact of writing textbooks on the prospects for getting tenure at your institution. Unless you get strong assurances from them that textbooks are acceptable for meeting publication and scholarship requirements, it would be safest to assume that they are not and not attempt to use them for this purpose.

There are at least three reasons why textbooks might not be regarded as acceptable for meeting publication requirements for tenure. The first is that writing them is not viewed as a scholarly activity. Lower division undergraduate textbooks are particularly unlikely to be viewed as scholarly. Although such textbooks might not be accepted as evidence of scholarship for a bid for tenure, they might be accepted as evidence of teaching excellence, particularly if they are based on courses you teach and have been widely adopted. Since the content of most college courses mirrors that of the textbook used, the fact that a course you developed is being taught elsewhere should be considered evidence of its excellence by the members of your promotion and tenure committee.

Second, textbooks routinely are not peer reviewed for scholarship. The reviewing that is done tends to focus mostly on their marketability. It can be argued that a textbook that is highly successful might not necessarily reflect a high level of scholarship. In fact, the opposite might be true.

A third reason why textbooks might not be regarded as acceptable for meeting publication requirements for tenure is professional envy and jealousy. Journal articles do not generate income for their authors. Academic books and professional books rarely generate much income for their authors. Textbooks, on the other hand, can generate considerable income for their authors. Consequently, textbooks are more likely than these other types of publications to trigger professional envy and jealousy.

For further information about textbook proposals and publishers, see Silverman (1998a).

### Trade Book Publishers

These companies publish nonfiction books for the general public. Some scientists and scholars write nonfiction books in which they translate research in their field into a form that can be understood and used by the general public. Scientists as eminent as Albert Einstein have written such books, as have many psychologists and medical researchers with university affiliations. Some books of this type have children rather than adults as their intended audience.

A scholar can make a significant contribution to society by writing a book of this type — perhaps even a greater one than writing a scholarly book. However, it is risky in most fields to use such books to support an application for promotion and tenure, particularly at universities that regard themselves as being research oriented. There are several reasons. First, they are unlikely to be regarded as works of original scholarship. Second, they are not peer reviewed. Third, they can trigger professional envy and jealousy because of the income they generate for their authors.

The amount of risk in writing a book of this type before receiving tenure can be influenced by several factors. One is the type of institution. It probably would be less risky to have a publication of this type on your record at a small liberal arts college than at a large research-oriented university.

Another factor that influences the amount of risk involved in writing such a book before receiving tenure is the remainder of your publication record. If aside from this book you have a solid publication record, a book of this type is unlikely to do you much harm. On the other hand, if you have done little or no publishing in peer-reviewed scholarly journals, a book of this type could do you considerable harm, particularly at a research-oriented university. Your promotion and tenure committee could view your writing such a book as evidence that, if you had wanted to, you could have been more productive as a scholar. It would be difficult for you to argue that your low scholarly productivity was due to your extraordinarily large teaching, advising, committee, or administrative responsibilities if you found the time to write such a book.

Writing nonfiction books of this type after you receive tenure can enable you to make a very significant contribution both to society and your college or university. With regard to the latter, such books can enhance the image (prestige) of an institution, thereby facilitating both student recruitment and alumni support. Benefits from this type of book publication are considered further in Chapter 12.

## Subsidy Publishers

These companies require an author to subsidize the publication of his or her book. They have little, or no, concern about the size of the market for a book or its quality because they make their money from its author. Consequently, they will publish almost anything. The copies they sell are mostly purchased by the author's family and friends. Occasionally, they do publish a book that sells a significant number of copies. However, this is an extremely rare event.

Although almost all subsidy publishers will publish a book by an academic author, a few appear to specialize in this market. They contact potential academic authors by direct mail advertising. They argue that traditional academic publishers do not publish all of the worthwhile books, particularly those that are unlikely to sell enough copies to be profitable. Consequently, by publishing such books they facilitate the free flow of ideas within the academic community. They also tend to offer authors a much higher royalty percentage than do other academic publishers. However, the amount that an author receives in royalties is highly unlikely to equal the amount the author pays as a subsidy to publish the book.

A book by a subsidy publisher can severely damage your prospects for receiving tenure. The imprint of the subsidy publisher you used would most likely be recognized by at least one of the persons who read your application. After this information was communicated to the members of your promotion and tenure committee, they would be likely to conclude that you were so desperate to get a publication that you were willing to subsidize it or your work probably had been rejected by legitimate academic publishers. Consequently, it probably has little merit. They, of course, would be less likely to grant you tenure after reaching such a conclusion than they would have been otherwise.

### Self-Publishing Option

Self-publishing is not subsidy publishing. The former has a long history of respectability and the latter does not. Books that were originally self-published include Mark Twain's *Huckleberry Finn*. They also include two of the best-selling textbooks in my field and an academic book that I authored.

There is, incidentally, one type of self-publishing that is widely accepted in academia — distributing copies of convention papers. Such papers are regarded as publications by U.S. copyright law. Consequently, they receive the same protection as other types of publications, regardless of whether a copyright notice appears on them or whether they have been registered with the Copyright Office at the Library of Congress.

Authors usually self-publish books under the name of a company they establish rather than their own name. (My publishing company is CODI Publications.) The cost of establishing such a company can be less than $500. Its mailing address can be a post office box. Self-published books can be listed in *Books in Print*, catalogued by the Library of Congress, and sold by college and trade bookstores. In fact, if a book is self-published under the name of a company, few people will view it as having been self-published. In this regard, it is worth noting that some major book publishing companies (including Prentice-Hall) were established to self-publish their founder's books.

Although self-published books and other projects can make a substantial contribution, they usually are not regarded as desirable for supporting a case for promotion and tenure, particularly if they have not been peer reviewed. If you are intending to use them for this purpose, it is crucial that you have them peer reviewed and include the reviews in your promotion and tenure document. A paragraph documenting the qualifications of each reviewer should also be included in the document. The reviewers should be scholars who have strong national or international reputations in your field. An assistant professor at my university successfully used this approach to document for promotion and tenure the scholarship in an oral history of jazz that he had self-published on audiotape. For further information about self-publishing, see Silverman (1998a).

## AUDIO, VISUAL, OR SOFTWARE PROJECTS

Options for PFT are not limited to books and articles. Although these are the most common media used for scholarly communication, there are others that can be appropriate, including audiotapes, videotapes, and CD-ROM disks or other computer-compatible media.

If you choose to use scholarly projects published in one of these ways to support your bid for tenure, you will have to show that they had been adequately peer reviewed. The presumption of at least some members of your promotion and tenure committee probably will be that projects published in these ways are unlikely to have been subjected to a rigorous peer-review process comparable to that for journal articles. If you cannot document that they were subjected to such a peer-review process, you will have to arrange to have them rigorously peer reviewed and include the reviews in an appendix to your promotion and tenure application.

These modes of publication and some scholarly projects that may be appropriate for each are dealt with in this section.

### Audiotapes

Academic publications on audiotape can mimic journal articles and books as well as communicate speech, music, and other sound-based material. Some are published by an entity other than their author(s) and others are self-published. Entities that publish audiotapes include academic, scientific, and professional associations and commercial publishers.

#### Audiotape Convention and Conference Proceedings

Audiotape publications that mimic journal articles include recordings of platform presentations and discussions at conferences and at academic, professional, and scientific association conventions. Copies can be ordered at the conference or convention and usually also by mail. The recordings can be made and distributed by the organization that sponsors a conference or convention or by a vendor that it contracts with before doing so. Such recordings usually are not peer reviewed before being sold. Although they can be an effective way to share information, they are not particularly helpful for supporting a bid for tenure unless they are peer reviewed.

### Audiotape Journals

There are journals in some fields that are published on audiotape. The articles in them are usually peer reviewed. The readers might not be the authors of the articles. Because almost all cars now have audiotape players built into their radios, these journals enable subscribers to productively utilize some of the time that they spend driving. You can use articles in audiotape journals to support a bid for tenure if you can document that they were peer reviewed.

### Audiobooks

Books on audiotape — audiobooks — are rapidly increasing in popularity. Some audiobook publishers are also print book publishers. Some audiobooks are voiced versions of printed books, and others are originals. Most are fiction or trade nonfiction. The acquisitions process used by audiobook publishers is the same as that used by print book publishers.

Audiobooks can offer several types of publishing opportunities to academics. One would be as an alternative to printed college textbooks, particularly ones that do not require graphs or other types of figures to convey information. Students are likely to spend more time studying audiobook textbooks than printed ones. In addition to studying them when they would study a printed textbook, they also can do so while doing something else, such as driving.

A second type of publishing opportunity that audiobooks can offer academic authors is books for scholars and other working professionals that do not require graphs or other types of figures to convey information. Such books can be originals or voiced versions of printed ones. They would be likely to be welcomed by busy working professionals because they can read them while doing something else, such as driving or exercising.

A third type of publishing opportunity that audiobooks can offer academic authors is books about aspects of their field intended for the general public. These can be either voiced versions of printed books or originals and are the equivalent of printed nonfiction trade books. Self-help audiobooks tend to be particularly popular. Unfortunately, audiobooks intended for the general public are unlikely to be particularly helpful for meeting the publishing requirements for tenure, particularly at universities that regard themselves as being research oriented.

## *Educational Materials on Audiotape*

Some information can be communicated more effectively by ear than by eye — that is, by including speech segments or music. Materials for foreign language and music appreciation courses would be examples. Some textbook publishers occasionally publish materials of these types. They can also be self-published. Publications of these types might not be particularly desirable to use for meeting publishing requirements for tenure (particularly at research universities) because of uncertainty about the rigor with which they were peer reviewed.

## Videotapes

Videotapes have been used as a medium for publishing both scholarly and educational materials. Such materials are most likely to be published and distributed by the institution that employs their author or authors. If you intend to use scholarly or educational materials on videotape to support your bid for promotion and tenure, it is critical that they be peer reviewed and the reviews be included in your application.

Videotape is a particularly good medium for reporting scholarly projects that require the viewing of short motion picture film or videotape segments to communicate clearly. An example of such a project could be one reporting the results of an experimental educational program. It may be possible to communicate aspects of the methodology used more clearly by showing them on videotape rather than describing them or illustrating them with photographs or drawings. Short segments of motion picture film, incidentally, can be copied easily on videotape.

Videotape is widely used for disseminating educational materials, including entire college courses (for example, the college courses broadcast by educational television stations). Its usage for this purpose is likely to increase considerably as distance learning grows in popularity.

## CD-ROM Disks or Other Computer-Compatible Media

Multimedia CD-ROM publications increasingly are being used for instruction at the college level. Entire textbooks and courses have been published on CD-ROM disks. Some college textbook publishers are publishing college textbooks or ancillary materials for use with them on CD-ROM disks. There also are some companies that specialize in publishing CD-ROM multimedia educational materials. If you intend to use such materials to support a bid for promotion and tenure, it is critical that they be peer reviewed and the reviews be included in your application regardless of whether they were peer reviewed by the publisher before publication. Because this type of publication is not widely accepted yet for supporting a bid for tenure, it is safest to have an overkill philosophy with regard to the amount of peer reviewing needed. You would also be wise to include in the application a paragraph for each CD-ROM disk specifying (documenting) the tasks that you did to produce it — for example, writing the text and roughing-out the graphics.

Computer programs intended for students or practitioners are another type of computer-related publication that has been used to support a bid for promotion and tenure. Textbook, professional book, and software publishers have published such programs. They have also been self-published. If you intend to use a computer program for this purpose, it is critical that it be peer reviewed and that you include the reviews in your application.

# 5

# Peer Review

> We all know that peer review is expensive, slow, prone to bias, open
> to abuse, possibly anti-innovatory, and unable to detect fraud. We
> also know that published papers that emerge from the process are
> often grossly deficient.
> — from a 1997 editorial in the *British Medical Journal*

Although the peer-review process for evaluating scientific and other
scholarly manuscripts, projects, and publications has some limitations
(see quotation above), its benefits are almost universally regarded as
outweighing them. Consequently, peer review is widely accepted in
academia. It is used by almost all print journals and many electronic ones
for making publishing decisions. It is used by some academic book and
material publishers for evaluating proposals and completed projects. It is
used by almost all granting agencies for screening research proposals for
funding. It is also used in several ways by promotion and tenure committees for evaluating candidates' publication records. Promotion and tenure
committees themselves are peer-review entities.

To win at the publishing for tenure (PFT) game, you are going to have
to cope successfully with the peer-review process. To maximize your likelihood of doing so, you need to understand how this process really functions. There is considerable subjectivity in it. By understanding the factors
that contribute to this subjectivity, you can maximize the likelihood of

having the process work for, rather than against, you. The information in this chapter hopefully will help you to both understand and cope successfully with the peer-review process.

## PEER REVIEWERS AS REFEREES

Throughout this book, we have been viewing PFT as a competitive game. Like most such games, it has referees. Referees enforce rules. When they detect what they believe to be a rule violation, they impose a penalty. The harshness of the penalty they impose for a violation is based on their judgment of its severity. If they regard a violation as severe enough, they can stop the game.

The referees in the PFT game are referred to as peer reviewers. They theoretically have the expertise to assess the value of the information presented in a manuscript or that which is likely to be generated by a project described in a proposal. The number of peer reviewers that evaluate a particular manuscript or proposal could range from as few as one to more than five, particularly if it is a grant proposal. Not all judgments of the referees may be given equal weight in publishing or funding decisions.

The persons who referee a particular manuscript or proposal could include the editor or grant administrator to whom it was submitted. An editor or grant administrator is likely to function as a peer reviewer if he or she considers himself or herself to be knowledgeable about the topic in a manuscript or proposal. In fact, he or she might be the only referee for a manuscript or proposal. This is particularly likely to happen if he or she considers a manuscript or proposal to be clearly inappropriate for the publisher or granting agency to which it was submitted.

Editors and grant administrators are not generally regarded in academia as being peer reviewers. In fact, manuscripts and proposals on which decisions were made solely by them are not usually regarded as having been peer reviewed. The truth is that they can often significantly influence the outcome of the peer-review process if they are highly motivated to have a particular manuscript accepted or rejected. There are several ways that they might be able to exert such an influence. One is through the selection of peer reviewers. An experienced journal editor, for example, is likely to know the likes and dislikes of the persons who could be asked to referee a particular manuscript and select ones who would be likely to react favorably or unfavorably to it. He or she can even solicit additional reviews if the ones received were not to his or her liking. Furthermore, he or she decides the amount of weight each peer review is given and whether the decision if all referees detect a serious problem in a manuscript will be a request for revision or an outright rejection.

## WHY PEER REVIEW

Whenever something is widely accepted and has been for a number of years, it is reasonable to assume that it is satisfying a need. With regard to peer review, the need being satisfied is a gate-keeping one — that is, selecting from the manuscripts and proposals submitted to a publisher or a funding agency the ones that are least flawed and, consequently, are most worth publishing or funding.

Before the twentieth century, editors and administrators of funding agencies usually made publishing and funding decisions. As the breadth of knowledge in almost all fields became too broad for any one person to master, editors and funding agency administrators began asking specialists to evaluate manuscripts and proposals. The specialists acted in an advisory capacity, and editors and funding agency administrators still took full responsibility for their decisions. With time, editors and funding agency administrators transferred a considerable amount of their gate-keeping responsibility to specialists, that is, peer reviewers.

People usually are reluctant to relinquish power unless they somehow find it advantageous to do so. One possible reason why editors and funding agency administrators might find it advantageous to relinquish some of their gate-keeping power is that they do not have sufficient time available to carefully evaluate all of the manuscripts or proposals they receive. Another reason is that they lack the expertise to judge the quality of most of those they receive. They, of course, do not have to relinquish power for these reasons — that is, they can have peer reviewers act in an advisory capacity. Perhaps the main reason for their willingness to relinquish their gate-keeping power — at least on paper — is that doing so makes them more comfortable. When they have to reject a paper or proposal or request extensive revisions, they do not have to assume total responsibility. They can transfer some or much of it to the comments and recommendations of peer reviewers. This reduces the likelihood that they will make enemies in the scientific or academic community from such publishing or funding decisions.

Peer reviewers usually remain anonymous to the authors of the manuscripts and proposals that they evaluate. The reason is a legitimate one — to enable them to be frank without fear of reprisal. However, as with most things in life, the anonymity of reviewers can have a down side. It can enable them to safely misuse their power — that is, to reject manuscripts and proposals that should not be rejected. They might do so for several reasons, including the following:

They do not consider the topic worthwhile.

They do not consider the topic to be of interest to a high enough percentage of the readership.

They dislike the authors or their affiliations.

The methodology used — though widely accepted — is different from the one they would use.

Acceptance of the authors' conclusions would cause the reviewers to have to change their beliefs.

They want to establish a reputation for themselves as having high standards.

They are having a bad day and need an ego boost.

Each of these is discussed below.

Reviewers can recommend rejecting a manuscript or proposal because they do not consider the topic to be worthwhile. There is probably no topic that would be regarded as worthwhile by all possible peer reviewers for a manuscript or proposal dealing with it. Even in a high interest area such as finding a cure for AIDS, a research proposal could be rejected because the majority of the reviewers who evaluated it considered it unlikely to yield enough useful information to justify its cost. They, of course, could be wrong. Furthermore, if some of the reviewers had been different, the panel could have recommended that the project be funded.

Reviewers for a journal can reject a manuscript and give as the reason that the topic is not of interest to a sufficiently high percentage of its readership. Although this can be a legitimate reason for rejecting manuscripts, it can also be a relatively safe way for reviewers to keep manuscripts that challenge (threaten) their beliefs from being published. Rejecting a manuscript on this basis does not require a reviewer to argue cogently against the author's conclusions or methodology. A reviewer is also unlikely to damage his or her reputation by doing so. The number of potential readers needed for an article to justify its publication is a highly subjective judgment with which others can disagree, but cannot label as wrong.

Another reason why reviewers might reject manuscripts or proposals when they should not is that they dislike their authors or their authors' affiliations. Some journals and funding agencies attempt to control for this type of bias by having manuscripts reviewed blind — that is, by removing the names of authors from the title pages, headers, and footers of manuscripts and proposals. Doing so, unfortunately, is not always successful in keeping the anonymity of the authors of an article. Because authors tend to cite their own publications in their articles, it is often relatively easy for a reviewer to guess who wrote a manuscript or proposal.

Reviewers also can inappropriately reject a manuscript or proposal because the methodology used — though widely accepted — is different from that which they would use. Researchers can reject a particular methodology for reasons other than it yielded data that lacked adequate levels of validity, reliability, or generality. Their rejection could be based on a hunch that the data it yields lacks an adequate level of one or more of these, even though they know of no real evidence that it does. Consequently, they would have used a different methodology.

Reviewers for a journal also could reject a manuscript because acceptance of its authors' conclusions would cause them to have to change their beliefs. Change of any type tends to cause anxiety and that which requires a person to modify one of his or her long-held beliefs can make that person extremely anxious. One way a person can cope with this source of anxiety is to find reasons to reject information that conflicts with his or her beliefs. If there is information in a manuscript that conflicts with a reviewer's beliefs, he or she might be strongly motivated to find reasons to reject the manuscript. I informally tested this hypothesis while I was associate editor for stuttering for the American Speech-Language-Hearing Association's main research journal. There are two schools of thought regarding the etiology of stuttering — one views it as physiological and the other as psychological. Manuscripts that supported a physiological etiology were more likely to be accepted by reviewers whose publications promoted a physiological etiology than by those whose publications promoted a psychological one, and vice versa. (I, of course, took this source of bias into consideration when making publishing decisions.)

Another potential source of bias for both manuscripts and proposals is a reviewer attempting to use the process as a vehicle for establishing a reputation for having extremely high standards. Such reviewers are likely to try to find reasons to reject rather than accept manuscripts. Their written evaluations of manuscripts are more likely to be negative than balanced. This type of bias is found most often in reviews by young scholars who are in the process of establishing a national reputation in their field.

There is one form of bias that can affect any reviewer. If the reviewer is having a bad day, he or she may seek an ego boost. One way to inflate one's ego is "to shoot someone down." If a manuscript or proposal is reviewed on such a day, the review is likely to be more negative than it would be otherwise.

## ALTERNATIVES TO TRADITIONAL PEER REVIEW

The review process for journal articles could change in the future. Alternatives and modifications are discussed.

### Using the Internet

One criticism of the peer-review process is that it takes too long to have manuscripts reviewed. Traditionally, the editor mails copies of manuscripts to reviewers who then mail their comments and recommendations back to the editor. E-mailing manuscripts to reviewers (possibly as attachments) or encouraging reviewers to e-mail their comments and recommendations can speed up the process. Some journal editors in my field have begun doing the latter. The use of e-mail reduces the time needed to review a manuscript by a week or so because e-mail communication is almost instantaneous. E-mail also makes the task of responding less formidable than responding by letter and, consequently, the reviewers are less likely to procrastinate.

### Having Manuscripts Carefully Scrutinized by Journal Editors

Although this process seems to give too much power to a journal's editor (or editors), it was being used by one of the most prestigious scientific journals, *Nature*, at the time this chapter was written. Articles that survive careful scrutiny by both editors and reviewers are likely to be better than those that are just scrutinized by reviewers. However, we all have biases and those of a journal editor could keep some valuable articles from being published.

### Having Manuscripts Graded by a Certification Panel

Articles would be submitted to a certification panel in one's field before being submitted to a journal. The panels — which would be established by scholarly groups and use the same kinds of experts that journals now use — would assign grades or stamps of approval to articles. Articles getting passing grades could then be submitted to print journals that accept the certification panel's stamp of approval. They could also be posted on a World Wide Web site (for example, that of an electronic journal) and skip print publication altogether. Under this plan, therefore, it is not necessary to have a paper published in a peer-reviewed journal to have it peer reviewed. Consequently, the plan decouples peer review from publishing. For further information about this proposal, see an article entitled "Provosts Push a Radical Plan to Change the Way Faculty Research is Evaluated" in the June 26, 1998, issue of *The Chronicle of Higher Education*.

## Letting Readers Sort Out the Strengths and Weaknesses of Studies

Peer review, with this alternative, occurs both pre- and post-publication. Journal editors are the prepublication reviewers and readers are the post-publication ones. Articles could be published as submitted or with changes suggested by editors. Reader reviews in print journals would be as letters to the editor and in electronic journals as e-mail messages appended to articles. This alternative was being used by at least one electronic journal, *naturalSCIENCE*, when this chapter was written.

## Prepublication Review via the Internet

Many scholars present prepublication versions of articles at conventions and conferences and distribute preprints to peers. They use suggestions from those who hear or read their articles to improve the articles before publication. Scholarly skywriting (Harnad, 1991) refers to using the Internet for preprint distribution and comment. Preprints of papers and comments pertaining to them are distributed automatically to a group of peers by means of an e-mail listserv to which they subscribe. Authors can include their e-mail address on their preprints if they want comments to be sent directly to them. If an article has a major problem, it is likely to be detected by such a prepublication peer-review process. If the problem is correctable, the revised manuscript is more likely than the original to be favorably received by the peer reviewers of the journal to which it is submitted.

A listserv might not be necessary to secure this type of prepublication review. You could send an e-mail message to several persons who are knowledgeable about the topic of your paper asking them whether they would be willing to informally review a prepublication draft. You would then e-mail copies to those who agreed to do so.

## PEER REVIEW FOR JOURNAL ARTICLES

Regardless of the limitations of the peer-review process, it currently is used widely and, consequently, you must cope successfully with it to win at the PFT game. There are things that you can do to maximize the likelihood of your papers surviving the peer-review process and getting published, which are now discussed.

### Submitting to Appropriate Journals

You can believe strongly (and perhaps correctly) that an article presents information that needs to be communicated to the readership of a particular journal, but if its reviewers do not regard the information as relevant to a significant percentage of its readership, the article is likely to be rejected. If a journal has published a number of papers with content similar to yours within the past year or two, its reviewers are likely to regard yours as appropriate unless, of course, they feel that the topic has been covered adequately. However, if no articles with similar content have been published during the past few years, there could be a reason other than none having been submitted. The biases of the editorial board or reviewers might have changed. If there is another journal that during the past few years has published articles with types of content that are similar to yours, you seriously should consider submitting your article to that journal, even if it is not quite as prestigious as the other. Your primary goal until you get tenure should probably be to develop an adequate publication record rather than to save the world. Of course, if you can make significant contributions to your field while developing an adequate publication record, so much the better.

### Submitting in the Specified Format

Almost all journals specify the format (for example, reference style) in which manuscripts are to be submitted. This information might be published in the journal or you can request it from the journal's editor. It is important to submit properly formatted manuscripts to journals for at least two reasons. First, journal editors tend to be overworked, and, if a manuscript is submitted in an inappropriate format, it takes less work for the editor to reject it than to work with the author to correct the format. Second, if an editor receives a manuscript in an inappropriate format, he or she is likely to assume that the manuscript was rejected by another journal. This is likely to cause the editor to evaluate the manuscript with a different mind set than he or she would otherwise, which significantly increases the likelihood of it being rejected.

## Writing Clearly and Minimizing Spelling and Grammatical Errors

A manuscript that requires considerable rewriting to get into shape for publication takes less work for an editor to reject than to fix. You should have one or more colleagues check your manuscripts for clarity and errors before submitting them.

## Submitting Articles of Appropriate Length

An article can be rejected by a journal because its length does not conform to the journal's standards — that is, because it is either too short or too long. Some journals, for example, rarely, if ever, publish one- or two-page articles as research reports. They might, however, publish them as letters to the editor. A relatively short research report, of course, can adequately communicate some findings and have as much impact as a relatively long one. For example, Benjamin Franklin's reports in the *Philosophical Transactions of the Royal Academy of London* of his lightning experiments using kites were relatively short. A journal that rarely, if ever, publishes one- or two-page research articles might not state this in its information for contributors. Before submitting a relatively short research report to a journal, examine some relatively recent issues to see they have published any research reports as short as yours. The reason they have not, of course, could be that none were submitted. If you are uncertain about whether a journal publishes short reports but decide to submit one anyhow, you might want to indicate in the cover letter that you are willing to have it published as a letter to the editor.

A research report is probably more likely to be rejected for being too long than too short. This is one of the most frequent reasons why I have recommended that an article be rejected. A relatively long article that reports a single experiment is probably more likely to be rejected than one that reports a series of experiments. Rejection for this reason is particularly likely from prestigious journals that have large numbers of submissions and a high rejection rate. A research report should be no longer than needed to clearly communicate what was done, why it was done, what was found, and possible implications of the findings.

Journals are particularly likely to reject long articles that appear to have been taken almost verbatim from doctoral dissertations. As much of a premium is not usually placed on economy of communication in doctoral dissertations as it is in journal articles. These differences in writing style are particularly likely to be evident in introductions (particularly literature reviews) and discussions. Consequently, considerable rewriting might be necessary to convert a dissertation into a journal article (or articles).

## Avoiding Antiestablishment Topics and Positions

Reviewers tend to represent the establishment and, consequently, they are likely to regard research that attacks their deeply held establishment beliefs as threatening. Therefore, they are likely to have a different mind set when reviewing such articles than when reviewing ones that do not do so — that is, they are likely, consciously or unconsciously, to try to find reasons to reject them. If you want to maximize your odds of developing an adequate publication record for promotion and tenure during your probationary period, you might find it prudent to delay writing politically incorrect articles until after being promoted and receiving tenure.

## Using Scientific Justifications that are Compelling

Reviewers are more likely to recommend publication for articles they regard as relevant than for those they do not. Although the relevance of a study reported in an article might seem obvious to its author, it might not be obvious to others. The reason for this difference is likely to be (at least in part) that its author has more knowledge of the literature that is pertinent to the study than most other scholars. Consequently, to maximize the likelihood that reviewers will understand the relevance of a study, the information that convinced the author that the study was worth doing should be at least summarized in the introduction to the paper. This has been referred to as establishing scientific justification for the study. You establish scientific justification by answering the "so what?" or "who cares?" question. You indicate why the study needed to be done — that is, summarize what you considered to be its theoretical and practical implications for scholars or practitioners. For further information about establishing scientific justification, see Silverman (1998b).

There is another tenure-related reason for clearly establishing the scientific justifications for studies. Scholars are more likely than otherwise to read research reports that they consider relevant to their interests and, consequently, they are more likely than otherwise to cite such reports. One of the ways that members of a promotion and tenure committee can judge the extent to which candidates have established a national reputation is to determine the number of times their papers were cited by scholars other than themselves. There are computer databases for many fields from which this information can be obtained fairly quickly.

## Using Methodologies that Reviewers Consider Appropriate

Some methodologies for studying a particular phenomenon tend to be regarded as yielding data that possess higher levels of validity and reliability than others. One of the most frequent reasons that reviewers reject research reports is that they question the validity or reliability of one or more of the methodologies used. The methodologies they question might yield data that have adequate levels of validity and reliability, perhaps even higher levels than the alternatives the reviewers would regard as appropriate. Nevertheless, because you are attempting to develop an adequate publication record for tenure, you would be wise to avoid controversial methodologies whenever possible.

One of the ways that you can get a manuscript rejected is to refuse to report some of the descriptive and inferential statistical analyses that reviewers regard as meaningful. You might not have done some of those requested because you did not consider them meaningful, and you might be right. However, if your goal is to get the manuscript accepted for publication and you are unable to convince the editor that analyses you did not do are unlikely to be helpful in understanding your data, you might want to consider including some of them if doing so would be unlikely to be regarded as inappropriate by readers. I have included statistical analysis that I did not regard as particularly meaningful in papers because publication was made contingent on their inclusion.

## Reacting Defensively to Editorial Comments

Scholarly, scientific, and professional journals rarely accept papers for publication as they are submitted. Some changes almost always are requested. Reacting defensively to an editor's request for changes in a manuscript could turn him or her off and result in the manuscript being rejected. If you believe that some of the changes an editor requests will result in erroneous information being communicated, you should present your reasons to the editor logically rather than emotionally. If after your doing so the editor still insists that changes be made, you probably would be wise to submit the manuscript to another journal.

### Revising Rejected Manuscripts and Submitting Them to Other Journals

Having a manuscript rejected is sustaining a loss, and whenever a person sustains a loss, it is normal for him or her to grieve. The grieving process has a number of predictable stages beginning with shock and denial, progressing to depression and anger, and hopefully ending with acceptance. Acceptance in the present context would be revising the manuscript (assuming it is salvageable) and submitting it to another journal. An article that has any merit at all is likely to be published eventually so long as you continue to revise and resubmit it. If there is a secret to developing an adequate publication record for promotion and tenure, this is it.

## PEER REVIEW FOR BOOK PROPOSALS AND MANUSCRIPTS

The peer-review process for book proposals and manuscripts is similar to that for journal articles except that considerable weight is given to marketability. A publishing contract is highly unlikely to be offered for a manuscript or proposal that reviewers do not indicate is likely to sell an adequate number of copies for the publisher to at least break even. Although this emphasis on the bottom line tends to be stronger for textbook and professional book publishers than it is for university presses, it is nevertheless still a consideration for university presses. It is crucial, therefore, that the presence of a market of adequate size be carefully documented when submitting a book proposal or manuscript to a publisher for consideration. There are suggestions for doing so in Silverman (1998a).

## PEER REVIEW FOR SCHOLARLY PROJECTS THAT EITHER WERE NOT REVIEWED BEFORE PUBLICATION OR FOR WHICH THE RIGOROUSNESS OF PEER REVIEWING COULD BE QUESTIONED

You might have scholarly projects that were either not peer reviewed or not rigorously reviewed before publication. These would include conference or convention papers; self-published reports, books, audiotapes, videotapes, and multimedia presentations on CD-ROM disks; and publications in electronic journals. Although the latter might have survived a rigorous peer-review process, electronic journals are so new to most fields that tenure committee members are apt to lack confidence in the rigorousness of the review process to which articles appearing in them are subjected before publication. It is important that you or someone in your department arranges to have them peer reviewed and that the reviews be included in your application for promotion and tenure. It is particularly important that this be done if many of your publications are of this type.

The persons selected to review such publications should be ones who are likely to be regarded by both persons outside of and within your field as being credible for doing so. Because the persons on your promotion and tenure committee who are not in your field are unlikely to be familiar with the persons who reviewed your publications, you should include a brief paragraph in the application about each that establishes his or her credibility for reviewing your publications. Because publications of these types are not traditional for supporting a bid for tenure, you would be wise to include in your application at least three credible reviews of each.

## PEER REVIEW OF PUBLICATION RECORDS

Some colleges and universities require peer reviews of the entire scholarly productivity of candidates for promotion and tenure. Copies of a candidates' journal articles, books, convention papers, et cetera are sent to several persons who are regarded as credible for doing this type of review. Candidates sometimes are asked to suggest persons. However, the persons they suggest will not necessarily be the ones selected to do the reviews. If asked to suggest persons to do the reviewing, you would be wise to suggest ones who have national reputations as scholars and are likely to value your research and other scholarly efforts. It is particularly important that you suggest scholars who are likely to value them if you are in a field in which there are several schools of thought about what constitutes worthwhile research.

# 6

# Creating an Article, Book, or Other Material

Remember that most successful writers compose their first three
manuscripts at four o'clock in the morning prior to a full day's work
in some office. If you can't discipline yourself to do that, you'll never
be a writer. Of course, it could just as effectively be after eleven
o'clock at night.

— Michener, 1992, p. 180

In this chapter we will focus on the process involved in creating an
academic article, book, or other material. The latter may be distributed on
paper, audiotapes, videotapes, or CD-ROM disks. Many aspects of the
process are described here, along with suggestions for coping (where
appropriate).

## FINDING THE TIME TO CREATE AN ACADEMIC
## ARTICLE, BOOK, OR OTHER MATERIAL

When you have a full faculty teaching, advising, and committee load as
well as family responsibilities, you are likely to have difficulty finding the
time to do the research and writing needed to develop an adequate publication record for tenure. Although you might intend to use summers and
vacations during the academic year for research and writing, you are

likely to find that family responsibilities or other personal commitments interfere, at least a little, with your doing so.

Relying on large blocks of time for research and writing can be risky for at least two reasons. First, there might not be enough large blocks of time during your probationary period to develop an adequate publication record by the end of it. Second, you might not have enough large blocks of time each year during your probationary period to publish sufficiently. Remember that tenure committees tend to be suspicious of persons who do most of their publishing a year or two before they go up for tenure. Furthermore, they are unlikely to accept as an excuse for having an inadequate number of publications the fact that you had a full faculty teaching, advising, and committee load during your probationary period — that is, no released time for research and writing. At least some of the members of your committee probably had a similar load during their probationary period and still found time to publish.

Fortunately, there is a way to find the time to do the research and writing needed to develop an adequate publication record for tenure. It requires you to establish a schedule that will enable you to work on projects at about the same time almost every day, for at least 30 minutes. Many authors, including myself, use this strategy. Even if your schedule only enables you to work on a project for 30 minutes daily, you can make significant progress.

The importance of a regular schedule — this same half hour every day—is vital; a definite rhythm is created both mentally and physically, and the writer automatically goes to his [or her] desk at that certain time, drawn by habit. The brain too . . . quickly learns to operate efficiently at such times. . . . Once the pattern of a daily half hour at a stated time is set, nothing short of disaster will keep you from writing. . . . The mere fact that such a routine is habit-forming . . . will condition you to greater output. (*Principles of Good Writing,* 1969, pp. 88, 91)

I have used this strategy for the past 30 years. It has enabled me to produce approximately 125 journal articles and 12 books while carrying a full faculty load. I write every morning (immediately after waking and having a cup or two of coffee) for 30 minutes to an hour. By doing so, I have been able to draft manuscripts for 300- to 350-page books in approximately 18 months.

One reservation that you are likely to have about this strategy is that you need time to think before you write and consequently, much (perhaps most) of each 30-minute period would be likely to be spent thinking. Although only a half hour might be scheduled for writing, the preparation for doing it is likely to take place all day. Somerset Maugham, the novelist, in an interview commented that: "The author does not only write while he's at his desk, he writes all day long, when he is thinking, when he is reading, when he is experiencing, everything he sees and feels is significant to his purpose and, consciously or unconsciously, he is forever storing and making over his impressions" (quoted in *Principles of Good Writing*, 1969). Several authors whom I interviewed made similar comments.

I write almost every night. And I think about it during the day and get thoughts organized in my mind so that when I come home I can sit down and actually do it. I have done a whole chapter in one sitting because I had it all in my head.

The book constantly is on my mind. How do I want to conceptualize this? Can I say it this way? In thinking about it, I found I was preoccupied by it almost 24 hours a day.

Although maintaining a daily writing schedule can make you more productive as a scholar, it also can be addictive. We increasingly are becoming aware that people can become addicted to an activity, and writing is undoubtedly an activity to which you can become addicted. If writing becomes a part of your daily routine, you are likely to experience a void after you finish an article or a book or if you are unable to maintain your writing schedule for a day or two. The resulting void in your daily routine can cause a sense of loss and grief. One phase of the grieving process is depression. As an interviewee commented: "Expect the postpartum depression syndrome when you send off the last chapter. The first time I had it, I didn't know what it was. I was just lower than a snake's belly." A person may attempt to cope with such depression by writing another book or article.

People can become so addicted to writing that they will knowingly write and submit material for publication that they know is not good. George Bernard Shaw (the playwright), for example, after turning out some awfully bad work in his nineties is reported to have indicated that he knew the work was bad but had become so addicted to writing that he could not stop (Krementz, 1996).

Becoming a little addicted to writing and publishing can be career enhancing for a scholar. However, if the addiction gets to the point where it compels you to submit worthless work for publication, you will need to do some soul searching and possibly seek professional help.

## WHERE AND WITH WHAT TO WRITE

There are several decisions you have to make before beginning to write. One decision concerns what implement you will use to write. Although almost all authors now use a computer with word-processing software, some still use a typewriter. Before 1980 almost all books and articles published during this century were written with a typewriter. I am mentioning this not because I advocate using a typewriter, but because I want you to be aware that you do not have to invest in a computer unless, of course, you are asked to submit the manuscript on disk as well as on paper. Actually, even if you are asked to submit a manuscript on disk, you probably could still use a typewriter and scan the pages into a computer using optical character recognition software. Although I now use a computer, my first four books were written with a 1950s vintage manual typewriter.

Most authors have switched from typewriters to computers for drafting manuscripts. There are several reasons. First, editing does not require retyping pages. Sentences and paragraphs can be added, deleted, modified, and relocated without having to retype them. Second, using software that checks spelling and grammatical usage and suggests synonyms can facilitate editing. Third, manuscripts for new editions are easier to prepare because material that is being retained does not have to be retyped. Finally, it is possible to edit and typeset from word-processor files. Authors who self-publish, incidentally, usually typeset in this way.

Although it is more efficient to draft a manuscript with a computer than with a typewriter, some authors, including James Michener, argue that doing so has the potential to adversely affect writing quality (Michener, 1992). They have indicated several reasons, the most cogent perhaps being the following. The quality of the organization in long article and book manuscripts is likely to be affected by doing all of the editing on a monitor screen (rather than on both a monitor screen and a printout) because you cannot view more than 25 lines at a time (unless, of course, you have a full-page monitor).

Some authors still do first drafts on legal pads. In one survey of college textbook authors during the early 1990s, 27 percent reported doing so. Several of the authors whom I interviewed commented that drafting in this way improved the quality of their writing because they found themselves considering alternatives to every word, phrase, sentence, and paragraph while they were keyboarding what they wrote. Furthermore, they indicated that they could work on their manuscript anywhere and for as long as they wanted. They were not restricted, for example, by the amount of power remaining in the battery of a laptop computer.

A considerable amount of the material that I wrote during the past 25 years was drafted initially on sheets of paper. The sheets of paper were sometimes in pads or three-ring binders and sometimes carried folded in a shirt pocket. I always edited the material while keyboarding it. Drafting material in this manner enabled me to work on a project wherever I was while traveling.

There, of course, are other ways to draft manuscripts. One of the authors whom I interviewed indicated that his way of doing it utilizes a tape recorder, a legal pad, and a computer.

The way I write is I think a great deal about what I'm going to write. And I'll be concentrating on a given subject area which will constitute a chapter eventually. And I keep thinking about that. And then I work up the illustrations — charts and graphs — and examples. Then, having done that preliminary work on the subject, I will dictate into a tape recorder the whole chapter at once around all of those examples and illustrations. I have a chapter. So, I play it back to myself and I write it down in longhand in pencil and I revise it as I write. Then I type the whole thing and I revise as I'm doing this. This is a real rough draft. Next, I retype it again in more finished copy. That's what the publisher gets. I have rewritten and retyped three times. That's exactly the way I write. I've done it all my life.

There is no one right way to write.

Another decision you will have to make is where to write. Some authors write at their office, some at home, and some at both. I do it at both. If you are using a computer and are planning to write at both your home and office, you will either have to have a computer at home that is compatible with the one at your office or a portable (laptop) one.

Some authors, including myself, occasionally write at other locations, including hotel rooms and lobbies, airports, and restaurants. I am an early morning person and when I travel, I usually write at a restaurant for several hours while having breakfast.

It is advantageous to be able to work on a manuscript wherever you are. You can take advantage of some of the small blocks of time that occur almost every day. They can occur at work between classes and/or meetings. They can occur at home when you wake up early or when you are tempted to watch television programs in which you really have no interest. They can occur while you are traveling. Even if they last for only a few minutes, you might be able to make significant progress on a project by utilizing them. "William Carlos Williams, the physician-poet, . . .

turned out a large body of work during office hours by writing *single lines of poetry between patients*. Williams kept pad and pencil in his desk drawer and between the time one patient left his office and the next entered, he would scribble a line—and sometimes two or more!" (*Principles of Good Writing*, 1969, p. 90).

When such blocks of time occur even though you do not have a computer available, you can write on a pad (or whatever paper is available) and keyboard the material later. The topic about which you write does not have to be one with which you are currently dealing. All word-processing programs enable you to write paragraphs in any order and later arrange them appropriately.

Few authors can be productive if they constantly are being interrupted. Creating an interruption-free environment in your home can be particularly difficult if you have young children. One of my interviewees attempted to do it in a rather novel way. "When my daughter was in fifth grade I did much of my writing at home and she would sometimes come in and interrupt me. Once to discourage her from doing it I said 'Becky, every time you come in here and interrupt me it costs me ten cents a word.' Well, she came in after that and said, 'I've got a great idea dad. Put *the end* at the end of every chapter and then you can make another twenty cents.'"

One final comment. As I have indicated previously (see Chapter 2), many authors (myself included) use rituals and totems to keep from becoming blocked. Such rituals and totems are likely to affect the device(s) with which an author writes, when an author writes, or where an author writes. I, for example, begin writing as close to 7:00 A.M. as possible, with a Macintosh computer, surrounded by a collection of more than 100 old cameras. Although relying on rituals and totems is likely to seem irrational to others, it can be a useful device for coping with writing-related anxiety.

## USING WORDS AND IMAGES TO COMMUNICATE

The primary objective of scholarly publication — regardless of whether the medium is printed journals or books, the Internet, audiotape, videotape, or CD-ROM disks — is communication in which both obscurity and ambiguity are minimized. A scholar's ability to impact on a field — and, thereby, develop a national reputation in it — is directly related to the clarity with which he or she communicates observations and hypotheses to students and scholars in that field. Some of the things that can impede your ability to communicate with minimal obscurity and ambiguity are described here.

## Using Jargon

Scholars, particularly those just starting out, might be tempted to use their writing to show that they have a large vocabulary and are acquainted with the jargon of their field. Their doing so is likely to impress some readers. However, it also is likely to reduce the clarity of their writing and, thereby, the likelihood that their observations and hypotheses will impact sufficiently on their field for them to develop a national reputation. Scholars who are self-confident usually try to avoid using jargon and other words that are unlikely to be familiar to their readers.

## Using Confusing Graphics

An old Chinese saying is that a picture is worth 10,000 words. The use of graphics (drawings or photographs) in articles or books is certainly justifiable if they enable you to communicate observations or hypotheses either more clearly than words or more clearly than words alone. However, graphics that do not facilitate communicating your observations or hypotheses can confuse rather than clarify. Such confusion can arise, for example, when the information in a graph is identical to that in the text. Readers are apt to wonder whether they are missing something. Confusion also can arise when an author does not make clear what readers are supposed to learn from a drawing or photograph.

## Using Too Few Examples

Examples (both graphic and word) can facilitate communicating observations and hypotheses. Authors might include too few for several reasons. First, they could feel that they used an adequate number of examples because the observations or hypotheses were clear to them. The problem is that they have information based on their readings or research that many (perhaps most) of their readers do not have. Consequently, although the examples are adequate for them, they might not be adequate for many readers.

A second reason why authors might include too few examples is fear of offending readers by questioning their intelligence. They might hesitate to include many examples because of fear that readers will regard them as being condescending. Some readers might view them in this way if they do not require all of the examples given to understand an observation or hypothesis. However, the consequences of not including a sufficient number of examples are such that it is safer to err by having too many than too few. One way, incidentally, of minimizing the likelihood of offending readers by including too many examples is to have several persons with whom you have not discussed your observations and hypotheses read the material and vet it for this possibility.

### Deviating from the Expected Format

Some scholarly writings tend to be organized in a particular way. For example, research reports in many fields are organized by title, abstract, key words, introduction, methodology, results, discussion, references, and appendixes. Using a different organization to report your research could result in confusion or an unwillingness of readers to invest the time needed to find certain information. Either could reduce the impact of your research on your field, and neither would be likely to enhance your reputation nationally.

### Writing in the Active Voice

You are more likely to get and hold a reader's attention when you write in the active voice. This requires the use of active rather than passive verb forms. A verb is active when the subject is acting and passive when the subject is being acted upon. The passive voice tends to be a roundabout way of expressing an idea. Consider the following pairs of sentences, the first of which is written in the passive voice and the second in the active one.

The ball *was hit* by the batter.
The batter *hit* the ball.

The workshop *was enjoyed* by the participants.
The participants *enjoyed* the workshop.

The second is shorter and more direct and, consequently, more likely to hold your attention.

### Making Vague Hypotheses and Conclusions

It is normal to want to avoid errors. One way to minimize the likelihood of making errors in your writing is by making your conclusions and hypotheses vague. Although doing so should reduce the number of hypotheses and conclusions in your writings that readers are likely to consider wrong, it is also likely to reduce the impact of your writings on your field and, consequently, the likelihood that you will acquire a national reputation through them.

One characteristic of the scientific method — known as comprehensiveness or scope of knowledge (Fiegl, 1953) — states that all hypotheses and conclusions should be regarded as tentative and subject to revision whenever new information becomes available. Therefore, all hypotheses and conclusions should be assumed to begin with the following phrase: "With the information I currently have available it seems likely that. . . ."

This characteristic of the scientific method requires you to regard the hypotheses and conclusions in your writings and those of others as tentative. Consequently, it requires you to respect the right of others to be wrong and to expect them to respect your right to be wrong. If the hypotheses and conclusions in your writings are reasonable, based on the data available to you, the losses you sustain by being vague are likely to far outweigh the benefits.

## STRUCTURING RESEARCH REPORTS FOR JOURNAL ARTICLES AND CONVENTION OR CONFERENCE PAPERS

There is a standard format in most fields for journal articles and convention or conference papers of a particular genre. One that conforms to this format is more likely to be accepted for publication or presentation than one that does not do so.

One format that varies little from field to field in the physical, biological, social, and behavioral sciences is that for research reports. I will consider their structure in detail because they constitute the genre that is used most often to support a bid for tenure in these fields. Although scholarly articles in the humanities usually do not use this format in its entirety, they do use some components of it.

The typical research report contains the following components, usually arranged in the following order: title, abstract, key words, introduction section, methods section, results section, discussion section, acknowledgments, references, and appendixes. The types of information that each is expected to impart are indicated below.

## Title

A title is very important. If the information presented in a research report is not indicated by its title, the report might not reach potential consumers, for at least two reasons. First, the title is one of the main sources of information used by abstract journals and computer databases to index articles for retrieval. If the title does not clearly indicate the content of an article, it is less likely than otherwise to be indexed properly.

A title is also important because people scan titles (in bibliographies, tables of contents, and so forth) to identify papers they wish to read. If the content of a paper is not evident from its title, the paper might not be read by persons who could use the information presented in it.

You should keep various things in mind when writing a title for a paper. First, you should use wording that indicates as unambiguously as possible the content of the paper, that is, the questions asked. The title should include both the specific population or populations studied (for example, adults over the age of 50 who have cerebellar ataxia) and what was studied (for example, the outcome of a particular therapy). Both types of information can be combined to form a title such as: Therapy X: Impact on Adults over the Age of 50 with Cerebellar Ataxia.

Second, be as concise as possible. All unnecessary words should be eliminated. Consider this title: A Study of the Impact of Therapy X on Adults over the Age of 50 with Cerebellar Ataxia. The first four words, "A Study of the," can probably be deleted without altering what the title is intended to communicate.

Third, order the words appropriately. The first word (or words) in a title should at least partially define the topic. Consider the two titles suggested in this section for a study of the impact of a therapy on persons over the age of 50 who have cerebellar ataxia. Even if the first four words of the second title were eliminated, the first would still be better than the second because it begins with a word that is more important for communicating the content of the paper — that is, the name of the therapy.

## Abstract

The abstract (or summary) should provide the reader (usually in less than 150 words) with concise information about the question or questions asked, the procedures used to answer them, the answers obtained, and how the answers were interpreted. In most journals, the abstract appears below the title. One of its most important functions is to indicate — in conjunction with the title — the content of the article to users of abstracts journals and computer literature-search databases.

There are two basic types of abstracts. The first (and most commonly used) summarizes the content of the paper — that is, the question or questions asked, the observational procedures, the observations made, the answers to the questions, and the interpretations made. Here is a representative abstract of this type:

The effect of adaptation on the masking of tinnitus was investigated. Six patients with tinnitus performed two 5-min tracking tasks, each replicated six times. The first task investigated the masking of tinnitus by tracking the intensity of a pure tone required to mask the tinnitus. The second task examined adaptation of a suprathreshold tone by tracking the intensity of a pure tone required for constant loudness. For 3 patients, the change required for constant loudness did not differ from the change required for constant maskability. For 3 patients, however, these two changes were different. Possible implications of these results for determining the locus of tinnitus and for the use of tinnitus maskers are discussed. (Penner & Bilger, 1989, p. 339)

The second type of abstract, which is used less often than the first, describes the content of the paper. It indicates the topics that were dealt with in the paper. This type of abstract frequently is used for relatively long papers where the content cannot be summarized in the number of words allowed. It also sometimes is used for one- or two-page papers because a long abstract could look ridiculous when printed in a paper this short. Here is a representative abstract of this type: "This paper describes a dimension of the stuttering problem of elementary-school children — less frequent revision of reading errors than their nonstuttering peers" (Silverman & Williams, 1973, p. 584).

When writing an abstract or summary, you should remember to indicate the content of the paper as accurately and completely as possible within the length (that is, word) limit imposed by the journal. Also, the writing should be as concise as possible. The most appropriate (for example, descriptive, concrete) words for conveying what you want to describe should be used. All unnecessary words should be eliminated. You might find it helpful to read a number of abstracts one after the other. This intensive reading should help you develop an intuitive feeling for how they are written.

### Key Words

These are short lists of words that some journals include in articles (usually under the abstract) to supplement, for indexing purposes, the information presented in their titles and abstracts. They are intended to assist persons who index articles for computer databases — such as Medline and PsycINFO — to do so appropriately. It is assumed that authors probably are more knowledgeable about the search terms (that is, words) that are likely to be used for locating information in their articles than are professional indexers.


## Introduction

In the introduction to a paper, you indicate what you were trying to do and why you were trying to do it. That is, you indicate the questions you were attempting to answer and why you felt it important to attempt to answer each. Doing the latter establishes a scientific justification for the study. Your reasons — that is, your scientific justification — might not be the only possible ones.

It is important to demonstrate as explicitly as possible the relevance of the research you are reporting — that is, the questions you are answering. You should indicate as many cogent theoretical and clinical implications of possible answers to your questions as you can. Lead your readers to the point where they would agree that the questions you sought to answer were worth answering. As mentioned previously, it is not safe to assume that readers will understand the implications of answers to questions without having these implications pointed out to them.

In the introduction you also review the literature that is relevant to the questions you were attempting to answer. Specifically, you indicate any data you are aware of that directly or indirectly suggest an answer to these questions. These data, of course, might suggest different answers to specific questions (which would make any answer to them equivocal). An investigator usually attempts to indicate in the literature review why the available data only permit the questions asked to be partially answered or why it is important to gather additional data so that they can be answered more completely. If, based on a careful review of relevant literature, it appears that no data have been reported that suggest an answer to the questions asked, this should be indicated.

Before you attempt to write an introduction, you might find it helpful to read a number of them, one after the other. Doing so could help you develop an intuitive feeling for how they are structured.

## Methods

In the methods section of a research report, you indicate who or what you observed and how you made your observations. You should describe both in enough detail that another investigator could replicate your observations. In cases when sufficient detail cannot be provided within the space limits imposed by the journal, an address can be included from which a more detailed description of the methodology that was used can be obtained. The address could be that of the author or of the American Documentation Institute.

What information to include in a methods section should be based on whether it is necessary to replicate your observations. If you feel that a given piece of information is necessary for replication, it should be included. If you are uncertain, it would be better to make the error of including information that is not essential than doing the opposite.

Before you attempt to write a methods section, you might find it helpful to scan a number of them in an issue of a journal in your field, one after the other, paying particular attention to how they are organized.

## Results

In the results section of a research report, you describe what was observed — that is, the observations that were made to answer each question. The observations should be organized and presented in a manner that should make the answer to each question fairly obvious to most readers.

In this section, you answer each question and report the data on which each answer was based. You usually do not interpret your answers here but in the discussion section. There are instances, however, when it is desirable to interpret answers while they are being presented. A combined results and discussion section can be used in such instances.

## Discussion

In the discussion section of a research report, you indicate possible implications — both theoretical and practical — of the answers you obtained. You indicate both the ways in which your answers appear to be consistent with existing theory and practice and the ways in which they raise questions concerning the validity of aspects of them. It is particularly important that you refer again to the implications that you mentioned in the introduction section to establish scientific justification.

Questions for future research are sometimes suggested in the discussion section. A study often raises more questions than it answers. By mentioning such questions and indicating why each would be important to answer, you can help an investigator who wishes to answer them establish scientific justification for doing so. That is, he or she can establish, at least partially, scientific justification by referring to your discussion section.

### Acknowledgments

The primary purpose of an acknowledgments section is to credit and recognize the financial and other support you received from individuals and organizations while doing the research and preparing the research report. Any financial assistance should be acknowledged, as should any persons who significantly contributed to the research by performing such functions as locating subjects, administering the experimental treatments, or assisting in the process of data analysis. Other persons you might wish to acknowledge are consultants, investigators who provided you with unpublished data, administrators who in some manner facilitated the research process, and persons who read the manuscript critically and offered suggestions for improvement.

Another type of information that may be presented in an acknowledgment section is the author's current institutional affiliation if it differs from that given at the beginning of the article. Some journals also include in this section the name and address of the person to whom requests for reprints should be directed.

### References

All papers and books mentioned in the paper should be listed here. Although there is no standard reference style, you should acquaint yourself with the style used by the journal to which you plan to submit the paper before preparing this section.

### Appendixes

Appendixes can contain unpublished documents pertaining to the methodology used for gathering data. An example would be an unpublished test or other assessment instrument. They can also contain raw data.

## PREPARING ARTICLES FOR
## ELECTRONIC JOURNALS

Articles for electronic journals are prepared in much the same way as those for print journals. They usually are submitted in both printed form and on disk if the journal peer reviews articles in the traditional way — that is, by mailing copies to reviewers. However, if the journal peer reviews articles on line, the editor might not request printed copies.

The article, if accepted, will be uploaded from the disk. Consequently, the journal is likely to specify how the file containing it should be formatted.

## OUTLINES

Good outlines help authors develop their thoughts logically. They also help them ensure that all relevant topics will be covered and that the presentation will not be repetitious. Furthermore, they help to make the material easier to read (because the writing has greater unity) and to keep the writing moving forward (by naming the next topic that is to be written about).

Software for outlining is readily available. Most word-processing packages (such as Corel, WordPerfect, or Microsoft Word) contain such software. Also, there are independent outlining programs available whose files can be read by a word-processing program. Most such software allows paragraphs, drawings, and tables to be included in an outline. Some also allow photographs, sound recordings, and videotape segments to be included. Consequently, an outline can serve as a database for storing material that is to be included in a manuscript. Text, tables, drawings, and photographs can be scanned into such a database.

If you use word-processing software with outlining capability, you should not have to rekeyboard the content of an outline. You probably can, by issuing commands, incorporate all or part of one into a manuscript.

Most authors revise their outlines while they are writing. New topics and better orderings of topics often occur to them while they writing. Consequently, the content of an outline should be regarded as tentative and subject to change throughout the period that a manuscript is being drafted and edited.

Outlining can be particularly useful for defining chapters for books and assigning topics to them. There are two basic approaches that can be used. One is to proceed from chapters to topics and the other from topics to chapters. The first ordinarily is used when books on the subject already exist, either in your field or related ones. You use their tables of contents as a starting point for yours and their indexes as a starting point for both identifying topics to discuss and assigning them to chapters.

The second of these approaches — proceeding from topics to chapters — usually is used when a book is the first dealing with a subject. You identify the topics you want to discuss and assign them to categories. From these categories you define chapters. A given category could be a portion of a chapter or an entire one. It is important when using this approach to be certain that there are no orphan topics. Their presence indicates that additional chapters are needed or that at least one existing chapter has to be redefined.

## WRITE FIRST, EDIT LATER

Once you have developed a reasonably complete first approximation of your outline, you should begin to write. The outline should be transferred to a word-processor file, assuming that you are using a computer to draft the manuscript.

As I have indicated previously, sentences and paragraphs can be cut from the outline and pasted in the manuscript. Doing so makes it unnecessary to rekey them. Illustrations and tables that were stored in the outline can be incorporated into the manuscript in this same way.

The attitude toward writing that is most likely to facilitate progress is viewing it as a two-stage process. The first is getting down what you want to communicate, and the second is revising (editing) what you have written so that your message will be clear to the reader. The following remarks by Roger H. Garrison (from *Principles of Good Writing*, 1969) indicate the importance of the latter: "Nearly all first drafts, even those of skilled writers, are verbose, awkward, and disconnected. Ideas have gaps in one place and overflow in another. Sentences and paragraphs are turgid and muddy. A first draft is like the slow emerging of a statue from a block of stone. The rough shape of the work may be plain, but there is much chisel work and smoothing to be done."

During the first stage, you should not be too concerned about word choice, spelling, grammatical usage, or sentence structure. If ideas occur to you for improving these, it is acceptable to do a little editing, so long as doing it does not interfere with getting down your thoughts. Most experienced authors do very little editing before they finish drafting a manuscript. However, if knowing there are lots of errors disturbs you and keeps you from moving forward, then do what editing you think is necessary.

The most important part of the manuscript-drafting process is the first — communicating your unique knowledge. Your manuscript will be judged primarily on the usefulness of its content to consumers. Although you certainly should strive to make the writing as clear and interesting as you can and the spelling and grammatical usage as correct as you can, the copyeditor can be expected to fill the gap if your efforts fall a little short in this regard.

Your primary focus while editing the manuscript should be to eliminate grammatical and spelling errors and to communicate clearly to your intended audience. The book by King (1991), although intended for physicians, presents suggestions that should help any textbook or professional book author to communicate more clearly. The book by Strunk and White (1979) can help you to identify and eliminate common grammatical errors. Other books on writing you might find helpful are those by Van Til (1986) and Zinsser (1988).

You should present your material as interestingly as you can. The amount of attention that people will pay to what you write will be determined, in part, by how interesting it is to them. Although subject matter certainly influences a reader's level of interest in a topic, the manner in which the topic is communicated does also.

There are several strategies that can be used to make material interesting to readers. One is to include as many examples as possible that both clarify concepts and are relevant to the readers' interests.

Another strategy that you can use to make material more interesting is to write in an oral style. There are several ways to achieve this. One is to dictate first drafts, using an audiocassette tape recorder or a dictating machine. Incidentally, if some of the topics about which you will be writing are ones about which you lecture, you may want to tape-record lectures in which you discuss them.

A second way to achieve an oral writing style is to read aloud what you have written. Visualize the audience to whom you are trying to communicate (for a textbook it would consist of students). If a sentence probably would sound awkward to persons in that audience if you were lecturing to them, change the wording.

## CHECKING MANUSCRIPTS FOR POLITICAL CORRECTNESS

Manuscripts to be politically correct must be free of sexism and sensitive to multicultural diversity. Both journal and book manuscripts should be as free of sexist language as possible. An example of such language is using the masculine pronoun (he or him) to refer to professionals in a particular field. As the McGraw-Hill Book Company has pointed out in its booklet, *Guidelines for Bias-Free Publishing* (pp. 11–12):

The English language lacks a nongender-specific singular personal pronoun. Although masculine pronouns have generally been used for reference to a hypothetical person or to humanity in general (in such constructions as "anyone . . . he" and "each child opened his book"), the following alternatives are recommended as preferable.

Recast to eliminate unnecessary gender-specific pronouns.
> NO — When a mechanic is checking the brakes, he must observe several precautions.
> YES — When checking the brakes, a mechanic must observe several precautions.

Use a plural form of the pronoun — a very simple solution and often the best.
> When mechanics check the brakes, they must observe several precautions.

Recast in the passive voice, making sure there is no ambiguity.
> When a mechanic is checking the brakes, several precautions must be observed.

Use *one* or *we*.
> When checking the brakes, we must observe several precautions.

Use a relative clause
> A mechanic who is checking the brakes must observe several precautions.

Recast to substitute the antecedent for the pronoun.
> The committee must consider both the character of the applicant and his financial responsibilities.
> The committee must consider both the character and financial responsibilities of the applicant.

Use *he or she*, *him or her*, or *his or her*. (These constructions have passed easily into wide use.)
> The committee must consider the character of the applicant and his or her financial responsibilities.

Alternate male and female expressions and examples.
> I have often heard supervisors say "He is not the right man for the job," or "She lacks the qualifications for success."
> I have often heard supervisors say "She is not the right person for the job," or "He lacks the qualifications for success."

There also are other suggestions in this booklet for eliminating sexism. For further help in doing so, see *Fields' Reference Book for Non-sexist Words and Phrases* (1987) and Miller and Swift (1988).

A related issue to which it is important to be sensitive while editing your manuscript — particularly if it is a textbook — is insensitivity to cultural differences. It is important that we not inadvertently bias what we write by our own culture-related values and beliefs. Furthermore, because textbooks transmit values as well as information, you might be able through your writing (particularly through your choice of examples) to promote increased sensitivity to and acceptance of cultural diversity.

## OBTAINING PERMISSION TO USE COPYRIGHTED MATERIAL

Many academic books and articles contain material (text or illustrations) from books and journals that are copyrighted. It almost always is necessary to secure the written permission of the copyright owner to reproduce illustrations. This is not the case for text. The reason is the doctrine of fair use — a component of the Copyright Act of 1976 (our current copyright law). This doctrine and other aspects of copyright law that are relevant for academic authors are dealt with in Chapter 8.

## ACQUIRING DRAWINGS AND PHOTOGRAPHS

Unless your project is a textbook for a large enrollment undergraduate course, you are likely to have to both provide and pay for illustrations (drawings and photographs). There are several suggestions in this section for doing so at relatively low cost.

You might be able to acquire some of the photographs and drawings that you need from professional books, journal articles, advertisements, and product catalogs. Some professional and scientific journals will allow you to use photographs and drawings from papers in them without paying a fee if the authors of the papers in which they appear are agreeable. Also, some academic and professional book publishers — particularly university presses — will allow you to use illustrations from books they have published either without cost or for a nominal fee. Furthermore, copies of photographs and drawings from advertisements and product catalogs often can be acquired and used without cost if their source is acknowledged.

Many illustrations in books and other printed materials are now created from drawings and photographs that are scanned into a computer and manipulated (retouched). The drawings and photographs scanned might be originals or from journals, books, or other publications. If they are from publications, they may be scanned directly from the pages on which they appear or from high-quality photocopies of them. Drawings that are scanned from publications usually reproduce closer in quality to the original than do photographs.

Once a drawing or photograph is scanned into a computer, it can be manipulated (retouched) in a number of ways. For example, its size can be increased or decreased. If it is in color, it can be converted to black and white. Its contrast can be increased or decreased. If it is a drawing, portions of it can be removed and new elements (for example, labels) added. If it is a photograph, a part of the image (for example, a distracting background) can be eliminated or a part of another photograph (for example, a more appropriate background) can be added to it. This, incidentally, is how the half human-half animal and other bizarre photographs that appear in supermarket tabloids are created. The sophisticated image-manipulation software that is currently available enables almost any modification to be made to a drawing or photograph. Someone who has little or no artistic ability can make many of these modifications.

### Drawings

There are two options for creating graphs and other drawings you are unable to acquire. You can have them created by a freelance illustrator from rough sketches or you can generate them yourself using a computer. Although the first of these options might (but not necessarily will) yield drawings that are more attractive than the second, it is unlikely to yield ones that are more accurate. In fact, a drawing that you create is more likely to communicate what you want to communicate because you know specifically what it should be and an illustrator might not. Another advantage of doing it yourself is that it is a lot cheaper.

Software is available for converting sets of numbers into graphs that are suitable for publication. Almost any type of graph can be drawn in this way. You supply the data and a description of the type of graph you want, and the computer does the rest. You can use either a program intended specifically for this purpose (for example, Datagraph Professional) or a spreadsheet program that has this capability (for example, Microsoft Excel). You can submit graphs drawn in this way as files on a computer disk, as laser or inkjet printouts, or both. Most publishers prefer to have graphs and other drawings submitted on disk because they do not have to scan them. If you hire an illustrator to draw graphs, he or she will probably draw them with this type of software. Consequently, they will be no more attractive (and possibly less accurate) than ones you draw yourself.

There is software available for making drawings other than graphs. There are several types of drawings that almost anyone can produce with such software after a few hours of practice. To produce charts (for example, flow and organizational ones) usually entails drawing some geometric shapes (for example, rectangles), arranging them appropriately on a page, connecting them by lines or arrows, and placing text in (or adjacent to) them to indicate what they represent. With a drawing program, such as MacDraw Professional, every element (geometric shape, connecting line, word) is a separate object that can be moved or modified without affecting other parts of the drawing. Consequently, mistakes can be corrected easily. Charts, like graphs, can be submitted on disk, printed on paper, or both.

Another type of drawing that requires little or no artistic ability to produce is one that is a slightly modified version of an existing drawing, particularly one that only requires you to remove (erase) elements or change text. The existing drawing is scanned into the computer and modified with a drawing program.

If the resulting drawing is quite similar to the original and you do not own the copyright on the original, you should probably request permission to reproduce the modified drawing from the copyright owner. I included the word probably because, if the drawing is a generic one, permission to reproduce might not be necessary. Unfortunately, there are no generally accepted guidelines for what constitutes a generic drawing. Consequently, even though it might not be necessary to obtain permission to reproduce a drawing that most people would classify as generic, it probably would be a good idea to do so.

You probably will have to rely on a freelance illustrator for complex drawings, such as anatomical ones. Producing them can be quite expensive.

## Photographs

There are several ways that you can get the photographs you need that are not available for free or a nominal charge from one of the sources previously mentioned. You could take the photographs yourself, have them taken by a professional photographer, or purchase them from an agency that sells stock photographs.

If you have access to a camera — such as a 35mm single-lens reflex — you should be able to take at least a few of the photographs you need. You also might be able to abstract them from videotapes that were made with a camcorder. The quality of the image will be somewhat better than the one you see on a television screen when you pause the tape.

If you need photographs of a general nature (for example, candid photographs of children) and are unable to take them yourself, it might be cheaper to purchase them from an agency that sells stock photos than to have them taken by a professional photographer. The larger ones have hundreds of thousands of photographs in their files. Some of them are listed in *Photographer's Market*, which is published by Writer's Digest.

Two other sources for photographs of a general nature (from 1860 to the present) are the Library of Congress and the National Archives. Both charge very little for them. An 8- by 10-inch black-and-white print from the National Archives cost less than $10.00 when this chapter was written.

If there are people in some of your photographs who can be recognized, you should have them sign a model release form. There is a representative model release form in Silverman (1998a).

## PREPARING CAMERA-READY COPY

Some journal and book publishers require authors to submit camera-ready copy. The process by which pages for almost all publications are now printed is a photographic one. The text and illustrations in a manuscript are laid out in pages and the pages (that is, the camera-ready copy) are photographed and printed.

The persons who create camera-ready copy for academic journals and books usually are not their authors. They are copyeditors, typesetters, and proofreaders. One way that a publisher can reduce expenses — and thereby make a project financially viable that would not be otherwise — is to have the author (or authors) do the copyediting, page layout (including typesetting), proofreading, and printing of camera-ready copy. An author is most likely to be asked to perform these tasks for a publication that is not expected to sell many copies — for example, a proceedings volume for a conference.

Computer software is available that can enable you to create fairly high-quality camera-ready copy from word processor files. A word processor's spelling and grammar checking capabilities can facilitate copyediting. A word processor's page layout capabilities are likely to be adequate to combine text and illustrations into pages for most academic publications. A page layout program, such as PageMaker, also can be used for doing so. Camera-ready copy (that is, pages) can be printed with an inkjet or laser printer. If illustrations are limited to line drawings, a 300-dpi printer can create acceptable camera-ready copy. For pages with photographs and drawings containing shades of gray, the output from a 1,200 dpi or better printer is desirable. Such a printer, if you do not have one, is available at some copy shops.

Preparing camera-ready copy can be time-consuming, but it is unlikely to require any ability you do not possess. Page layouts tend to be relatively straightforward, and publishers usually provide detailed instructions for creating them.

## PREPARING MATERIALS FOR AUDIOTAPE, VIDEOTAPE, AND CD-ROM PUBLICATIONS

If you are not self-publishing and your publication is not a recording of a lecture or presentation, you are unlikely to be responsible for creating the master for your audiotape, videotape, or CD-ROM publication. However, you will be responsible for preparing the script and possibly a storyboard for it. In addition, you might be asked to provide some drawings, photographs, audiotape segments, or videotape segments for it.

The author is responsible for drafting the script for all three types of publications. The script, like that for a play, will contain dialogue and possibly also directions for staging. For audiobook (audiotape) publications, this is likely to be the author's primary responsibility. For videotape and CD-ROM publications, the staging directions in the script are likely to be supplemented by a storyboard. A storyboard consists of a series of rough sketches depicting the graphics (drawings, photographs, animations, and so forth) in a publication, arranged in the appropriate sequence. The script and storyboard are used as a guide by the team that produces the master for the videotape or CD-ROM publication.

Authors of CD-ROM publications (as well as most other computer software) are not expected to write computer code for them. They are just expected to provide a script and a storyboard that show the content of the various screens the software must generate.

## AN AUTHOR'S RESPONSIBILITIES DURING PRODUCTION

After your manuscript or other project is accepted for publication, you are not done with it. You will have at least one more responsibility before it is published — checking proofs. You will receive a copy of the page proofs for your book or journal article or the master for your audiotape, videotape, or CD-ROM publication to check for errors that were introduced during production. They should be checked carefully. The page proofs for most of my journal articles and those for all of my books contained such errors.

Authors of books are likely to have at least two other responsibilities during production — checking the copyedited manuscript and indexing. After a book manuscript is put into production (launched), it is copyedited. The copyeditor adds typesetting instructions to it and attempts to correct spelling and grammatical errors and otherwise improve the writing. At least a few of the changes that a copyeditor makes to improve the writing in a book manuscript are likely to affect meaning. Few book manuscripts are copyedited by persons who are knowledgeable about the topics that are discussed in the book. It is not surprising, therefore, that a copyeditor could change the meaning of an awkward sentence when rewriting it without realizing that he or she is doing so. Consequently, it is crucial that you carefully check all of the changes that the copyeditor made in your manuscript to make certain that they do not affect meaning. You should certainly attempt to rewrite awkward sentences. However, if you cannot improve them, it is better to have awkward sentences that accurately communicate meaning than well-written ones that do not do so.

You also should carefully check the copyedited manuscript for errors that you made and for errors of omission (topics that should have been discussed, but were not). Some of your errors might not have been errors when you wrote the material but are now because new information became available. If changes have to be made, they should be made in the manuscript — before it is typeset. Changes made in the page proofs not only are expensive but they can affect the accuracy of the index because the book will be indexed from the page proofs.

Another responsibility that you are likely to have during production is creating the index for the book. Although a professional indexer could index your book, you might want to do it yourself for at least two reasons. First, the indexer's fee will probably be deducted from your royalties. Second, the indexer is unlikely to be highly knowledgeable about the topics dealt with in your book and, consequently, he or she is likely to leave out some that would be of interest to readers. It is not difficult to index an academic book, and there are detailed instructions for doing so in Silverman (1998a).

## SELF-PUBLISHING

When you self-publish, you assume responsibility for all of the tasks required to produce and market a book, educational or professional material (for example, a psychological test), or a publication on audiotape, videotape, or CD-ROM disks. You can do all of them yourself or contract with others to do some of them. Few publishers, incidentally, do all production tasks in house. They use others for doing most of them, including copyediting, drawing figures, cover design, typesetting, proofreading, printing, and binding. You could, if you wanted to, use the same freelancers and firms. Consequently, your publications could be of the same quality as those produced by other publishers.

There is practical information about the production tasks for self-publishing in Silverman (1998a).

## POST-PUBLICATION RESPONSIBILITIES

Your post-publication responsibilities will depend on the type of publication that it is. If it is a journal article, a convention paper, or an audiotape or videotape of lectures or other presentations, your responsibilities will be pretty much limited to filling requests for copies. In contrast, if it is a book, educational or professional material, audiobook, or multimedia CD-ROM production, you are likely to have several responsibilities. One is to assist in marketing the publication. This could be limited to completing a marketing questionnaire for the publisher. A second would be to periodically revise the material (assuming that it sells enough copies to justify it being revised). A third is to answer purchaser's content-related questions.

# 7

# Submission Strategies

> The sooner you send your material out, the sooner you'll get your
> first rejection slip and, with it, the first layer of thick hide required to
> persevere in the impersonal world of the written word. The sooner,
> too, you'll get your first acceptance.
> — Allison & Frongia, 1992, p. 91

To win at the publishing for tenure game you must find publishers for the
papers and other scholarly work you have written. These publishers must
be journals or other firms that the members of your promotion and tenure
committee are likely to regard as being adequately prestigious and, at the
same time, are likely to facilitate your ability to establish a good national
reputation as a scholar.

Although being published by highly prestigious publishers is certainly
desirable, it is not essential. An article in a less prestigious journal can
also be helpful for achieving tenure if the journal uses a peer-review
process to select articles for publication. A publication in *The New
England Journal of Medicine* or *The Journal of the American Medical
Association* would probably be regarded as more prestigious than one in a
state medical journal. However, a publication in a state medical journal is
also likely to be helpful for achieving tenure if manuscripts submitted to it
are peer reviewed.

Your goal should be to get an adequate number of publications by the most prestigious publishers who are likely to be interested in your scholarly work. Submission strategies for achieving this goal will be discussed in this chapter. These submission strategies will focus on maximizing the likelihood that you will place your articles and other scholarly projects with publishers with whom the members of your promotion and tenure committee are likely to be impressed and, at the same time, ones that are likely to have a readership that will facilitate your establishing a national reputation as a scholar.

As the quotation at the beginning of this chapter indicates, an article or other publishable project submitted to an academically respectable journal or publishing firm (particularly a prestigious one) is more likely to be rejected than accepted. However, if you develop a thick hide and are persistent, the probability is high that your articles and other scholarly projects eventually will be accepted for publication.

## SUBMISSION STRATEGIES
## FOR JOURNAL ARTICLES

There is usually more than one journal for which a particular paper would be appropriate. It is not regarded as ethical to submit a paper to more than one journal at a time. Consequently, you will have to decide to which journal you will submit the paper first, and if necessary, second, third, fourth, and so on. A number of factors that you should consider when making this decision are discussed in this section.

### The Prestige of the Journal

Everything else being equal, you probably would want to submit articles first to the most prestigious journals for which they are appropriate. You might find it advantageous to do this even if everything else is not equal. This is particularly likely to be the case for prestigious journals that tend to make publishing decisions fairly quickly. Even if a paper stands only a very small chance of being accepted by such a journal, it would probably be advantageous to submit the paper to it first as long as doing so would not place you at significant risk for having an inadequate publication record when you apply for tenure. Consequently, this submission strategy would tend to be less risky at the beginning than at the end of your probationary period. Furthermore, it would tend to be less risky to your ego if you have developed a thick hide because rejection is a more likely outcome than acceptance.

## Each Journal's Rejection Rate for Articles

Journals vary considerably with regard to the percentage of submitted manuscripts that they accept. High-prestige journals tend to have higher rejection rates than low-prestige ones that publish the same number of pages a year. The main reason is that high-prestige journals tend to have more articles submitted to them than low-prestige ones.

## Review Time for Articles

Journals vary with regard to the number of months that it usually takes them to review articles. How long it takes does not appear to be related to how prestigious the journal is. Because it is not considered ethical to submit articles to several journals simultaneously, you might want to try to avoid journals that tend to be very slow.

There are several ways that you can get some information about how long it usually takes a journal to review an article. Some journals indicate for each article the date it was received and the date it was accepted. Examining several recent issues of a journal that provides this information should give you some idea of how long the review process is apt to take. If a journal does not provide this information, you might be able to get it by e-mailing or phoning persons who have recently published in the journal.

## The Journal's Editorial Board

If the journal editor is a friend, you are more likely to get an article accepted than if he or she is an enemy. Editors select the referees to whom articles are sent for peer review and they are likely to be aware of the theoretical and methodological biases of most of them. Consequently, an editor can increase the odds of an article being recommended for acceptance by having it refereed by persons who share the author's theoretical and methodological biases and reduce the odds of it being recommended for acceptance by having it refereed by persons who do not share them.

Even if you do not know the editor of a journal, this consideration could still be relevant. There might be persons on the editorial board who are likely to be consulted about your article who you know do not accept your theoretical positions or have questioned in their publications the validity or reliability of some of your methodology. You might want to avoid submitting your article to that journal if there are viable alternatives.

## Page Charges and Reprint Costs

Some journals have page charges that are either mandatory or voluntary. The payment of mandatory charges is a requirement for publication. Even though the payment of voluntary page charges is not a requirement for publication, you are expected to pay them if your research is supported by a grant that funds publication expenses.

You are likely to receive requests for reprints. Journals vary considerably with regard to how much they charge for them. Everything else being equal (which rarely happens), you might want to submit an article first to the journal for which it is appropriate that charges the least for reprints. You would probably only want to consider this factor if you do not have a grant that pays for reprints and neither your department nor graduate college pays for them.

## Appropriate Audience for the Article

Hopefully, your publications, in addition to getting you tenure, will do some others some good. The others could be scholars who are doing research in the same area or a related one. If you are in a helping field (for example, education, clinical psychology, or medicine), the others might be children or adults who could be helped by the information in your publications if those who are working with them are aware of it. Consequently, it is desirable that you publish in journals that are read by persons who can utilize the information from your publications.

The journal that is most likely to reach a large number of persons who could benefit from the information in an article might not be the most prestigious one for which the article would be appropriate. For example, an article informing speech pathologists in Wisconsin about new telephone services available there for persons who are speech or hearing impaired would be more likely to be helpful if it were published in the Wisconsin Speech and Hearing Association's newsletter than it would be if it were published in a high-prestige international speech pathology journal. A publication in the international journal is likely to contribute more to an application for tenure than one in a state association newsletter.

You might not be able to reach all of the persons who could benefit from the information you have to report with a single publication. The information might, for example, be helpful to scholars in a number of countries and there is no one journal through which you are likely to reach most of them. It also might be of interest to scholars in several fields and there is no one journal that most scholars in these fields are likely to read.

Worse yet, it could be that scholars in different fields who study the phenomenon use different terminology to describe it. Consequently, to be maximally helpful you would have to report the information in more than one journal and possibly present it in more than one way. Unfortunately, some members of your tenure committee might interpret your publishing essentially the same thing several times as an attempt to inflate your publication record. It is crucial, therefore, that, if you report similar information in several articles, you include a statement in your tenure application explaining why you did so.

## Readership of the Journal

Few, if any, scholars can find the time to regularly read every journal in their field. However, most are likely to read several regularly, including ones published by their professional association. For you to begin to develop a national reputation as a scholar it is necessary that others in your field—including ones who are not researching the same problem that you are—begin to associate your name with a specific scholarly domain within the field. This is most likely to happen if you publish in journals that large numbers of persons in your field are likely to at least skim regularly. These are most likely to be journals that are published by your professional association.

One strategy that some persons use to help them to become identified as an expert in a particular domain is to send reprints of articles they publish in that domain to other scholars who research it. They are particularly likely to send such scholars reprints of articles that are published in journals they are unlikely to read regularly. They also might send them relevant unpublished articles, including convention or conference papers and preprints of papers that are in submission or in press. By doing so, they are likely to increase both the number of times their papers get cited and the likelihood of their being invited to participate in conferences and contribute chapters to books.

## The Journal's Flexibility with Regard to Copyright

Many journal editors routinely ask authors to sign a form that transfers ownership of their article (that is, the copyright) to the journal. Signing this form has several consequences. First, it restricts an author's ability to include some of the sentences and paragraphs in the article in another for a different audience. As I have indicated elsewhere in this chapter, it might be necessary to report information in more than one journal to reach those who could use it.

A second consequence of transferring ownership of your article to a journal is a financial one. Persons who request permission to include an article in a course package for a class or a book of readings usually are charged a fee. Some journals print this fee on the articles in them. When you transfer ownership of an article to a journal, you cancel its obligation to share permission fees with you.

All that a journal really needs to publish an article is either first North American serial rights or first international serial rights. Journals vary with regard to their willingness to publish articles for which the author is only willing to grant these rights. If an article is highly unlikely to be included in a course package or book of readings and it is not necessary to publish the information in it elsewhere, then it probably would not be worthwhile to negotiate for something less than a copyright transfer. However, if an article is one that is likely to be included in course packages or books of readings or contains information that you might want to report elsewhere, you should definitely consider the willingness of the journals for which it would be appropriate to accept less than a copyright transfer when deciding where to publish it. You are, of course, more likely to be successful in getting an editor to accept less than a copyright transfer if you stress your possible need to include material from the article in other publications rather than your desire to benefit financially from permission fees.

### Databases that Abstract Journals

Important tools that scholars now use for doing literature searches are computer databases (for example, Medline and PsycLit). Few, if any, computer literature databases routinely abstract all of the journals that could contain relevant articles. Articles that are not abstracted in such databases are less likely to be read and cited and, consequently, are less likely than otherwise to contribute to your developing a national reputation. It is important when selecting a journal for an article, therefore, to determine whether the journal routinely is abstracted by relevant databases. A quick way to find out if a particular database routinely abstracts a journal is to search for articles in it that were published in the journal between three months and a year ago. Doing so, incidentally, can also give you some idea of how long it takes for an article to be abstracted by a particular database.

## The Number of Libraries that Subscribe to a Journal

The more libraries there are that subscribe to a journal, the more likely the articles in it are to be read and cited. Although copies of articles published in almost any journal can be obtained through interlibrary loan, only the most highly motivated scholars are likely to request copies from this source, and then only for articles that they know they have to read. You are most likely to read an article that does not appear from the abstract to be highly relevant to your research but could be if the journal in which it is published is readily available to you.

This issue, of course, is not relevant if you are publishing in electronic journals. Any computer that can access the Internet can access your articles.

## The Likelihood of Your Article Being Cited

Articles published in some journals are more likely to be cited than those published in others. Some factors that can affect the likelihood of an article being cited if it is published in a particular journal include:

the number of scholars who regularly read the journal who write articles for which the information in it is relevant;

the number of databases that abstract the journal; and

the prestige of the journal.

There are, of course, other factors that affect the likelihood of an article being cited, including the total number of scholars who are writing articles for which its content is relevant. The content of some articles has broader implications than that of others.

## Geographical Distribution of Readership

Some scholars become known nationally or internationally as well as in their state. If you publish almost exclusively in state journals, you are less likely to develop a national reputation than if you usually publish in national or international journals. Of course, if the information in an article is primarily of interest to persons in your state, it would probably make more sense to publish it in a state journal than in a national or international one.

## Policy Toward Negative Letters to the Editor

Most scholarly journals encourage readers to comment on articles through letters to the editor. Although it is certainly desirable for readers to have the opportunity to do so, journals vary with regard to the opportunity they give authors to respond to criticisms in them. Some journals routinely give an author an opportunity to respond to such criticisms and print his or her responses in the same issue as the letter to the editor. Others either do not routinely give authors the opportunity to respond to negative comments in letters to the editor or print responses in a later issue. The delay between the publication of the letter to the editor and the response could be six months or longer.

If an article is not traditional with regard to either conclusions or methodology, you will definitely want to publish it in a journal that routinely gives authors the opportunity to respond to critical comments in letters to the editor in the same issue. Such journals are desirable for other articles as well. I have, for example, been criticized for using a methodology that has been used by thousands of scholars during the past 50 years for the purpose that I used it. The person who criticized me was not familiar with the literature concerning this methodology. Because many readers were probably also unfamiliar with it, this letter could have damaged my reputation if I had not had the opportunity to respond in the same issue.

## The Journal's Peer-Review Process

Almost all scholarly journals use a peer-review process to select articles for publication (see Chapter 5). There is, however, considerable variation with regard to the nature of this process. Some of the ways that peer-review processes vary include:

the average length of time that it takes,

the number of persons who routinely review each manuscript,

the nature of the report requested from reviewers,

whether manuscripts are reviewed blind,

whether reviewers tend to be established scholars, and

how the editor uses reviewer comments when making publishing decisions.

Some implications of each are indicated in the paragraphs that follow.

Because you cannot make simultaneous submissions of manuscripts for journal articles, the length of time a journal's review process takes can be an important consideration when attempting to develop an adequate publication record for tenure, particularly near the end of your probationary period. In my experience, a journal review process can take as little as a few weeks to more than a year. It is a particularly important consideration if you are submitting to journals that have low acceptance rates—that is, ones that reject many more manuscripts than they accept. Several strategies for estimating the length of the review process are described elsewhere in this chapter.

The number of referees who routinely review each journal manuscript usually ranges from one to three. The more referees that review a manuscript, the less likely that one with an ax to grind will cause it to be rejected. Also, if the manuscript is rejected more referees are likely to give you the feedback you need to improve it sufficiently to be accepted elsewhere.

Journals also vary with regard to the nature of the report that they ask reviewers to submit. It can vary from a statement recommending publication as is, publication with revision, or rejection to completion of a form on which reviewers are asked to comment about a number of attributes of the manuscript or project reported in it. These attributes are likely to include the adequacy of the writing, literature review, and methodology and the contribution that its publication would be likely to make. Reviewers with an ax to grind are less likely to cause a manuscript to be rejected if they are required to justify their criticisms.

Some journals attempt to conceal the authorship of a manuscript from reviewers. This is referred to as blind reviewing. Although the attempt to keep an author's reputation (or lack of one) from influencing a review is commendable, it is not always successful. One reason is that academic authors tend to cite their previous publications. Another reason is that the scholars in a field tend to be familiar with what other active scholars in that field are researching.

Some journals use as reviewers established scholars almost exclusively and others use mostly scholars on their way up. The former are more likely to be motivated to help scholars who are at the beginning of their career than are the latter. Consequently, they are more likely than the latter to recommend that a manuscript be published. There are at least two reasons. First, a scholar at the beginning of his or her career is more likely to be viewed as a threat by someone who is not yet firmly established as a scholar than by someone who is. Second, a young scholar could attempt to find things wrong with a manuscript in order to impress the editor (probably an established scholar) and thereby advance his or her career.

The weight that an editor gives reviewers' comments and recommendations when making publishing decisions can vary from very little to considerable. If an editor does not like a manuscript and at least one reviewer did not like it either, this review can be used as an excuse for rejecting the manuscript without the editor having to forfeit his or her status as a good guy. In contrast, if an editor likes a manuscript, but one or more of the reviews are negative, he or she can either ignore them or get more reviews.

## SUBMISSION STRATEGIES FOR MATERIALS OTHER THAN JOURNAL ARTICLES

There usually is more than one publisher for which a particular project would be appropriate. Unlike submissions to journals, it is regarded as ethical to submit a project—usually as a proposal—to more than one publisher at a time. Publishing contracts for these types of projects are usually awarded from a proposal and one or two sample chapters or their audiovisual equivalents. For practical information about preparing this type of proposal, see Silverman (1998a).

There are both advantages and disadvantages to submitting a proposal to a number of publishers simultaneously. Advantages include getting a contract sooner and getting better contract terms (including a higher royalty percentage) if more than one publisher is interested in the project. A disadvantage is that if something is wrong with how the proposal is written, you could have the project rejected by all of the publishers for whom it would be appropriate. In contrast, if you only submit the proposal to one publisher at a time and it is rejected, you can use the reviewers' comments to modify the proposal before submitting it to another publisher. There is a candid in-depth discussion of these two submission strategies in Silverman (1998a).

If you use the sequential rather than the simultaneous submission strategy, there are a number of factors you might want to consider.

### Type of Publisher

Any type that would be appropriate should be considered except for subsidy publishers, who require authors to subsidize the publication of their works. They will publish almost anything that an author will pay to have published and usually make little or no attempt to market their books. Having a book published by such a firm is unlikely to impress the members of your tenure committee. In fact, it is likely to have the opposite impact on them.

Subsidy book publishers now operate on the Internet. You send them a publication fee and the pages of your book on disk. They upload the file to their site on the World Wide Web and persons order copies by paying a fee to download it. Because they (like traditional subsidy publishers) will publish almost anything, books published by them are unlikely to be helpful for achieving tenure.

The only type of publication subsidy that is academically respectable is an author's subvention paid to a university press. University presses sometimes expect authors to partially subsidize the publication of their books, particularly ones for which the market is likely to be small. This type of publication subsidy is academically respectable because university presses almost always subject manuscripts to a rigorous peer-review process.

### Reputation of the Publisher, Particularly in Your Field

It is desirable, but not essential, for the publisher to be one that has published books by well-known and respected scholars in your field. It is essential, however, that the firm is one that is likely to be respected by the members of your tenure committee.

### Publisher's Marketing Ability

Publishers vary with regard to their ability to successfully market particular types of projects. The ways in which it is most appropriate to market a book or other publication depends somewhat on the audience for which it is intended. Most publishers focus their marketing efforts on a limited number of audiences to keep from spreading themselves too thin. They either will not publish projects that they are unable to market adequately or they will publish them and hope that their usual marketing strategies will be adequate. Large college textbook publishers, for example, usually do not market books aggressively to working professionals. Consequently, if the audience for a book is mainly working professionals and graduate students, you will probably sell more copies if the book is published by a professional book publisher rather than a college textbook publisher. In contrast, if your book is a text for a large-enrollment undergraduate course, it would be a mistake to place it with a publisher that does not market college textbooks aggressively.

## Size of the Publisher

Large book publishers tend to invest most of their marketing budget in books that have the potential to sell large numbers of copies—that is, become best sellers. Consequently, a book that is not regarded as having this sales potential probably will not be marketed as aggressively as one that is thought to have it. This, of course, can result in a self-fulfilling prophecy—the book not selling well.

If your book is likely to be regarded as having the potential to sell huge numbers of copies, you probably should try to place it with a large publisher. If, however, it is unlikely to be regarded as having this potential, you probably will be better off placing it with a smaller publisher. Although a small publisher might not have books that sell huge numbers of copies, your book could be regarded by one as having the potential to become a best-seller. A book that sells 2,000 copies a year could be a best-seller for a relatively small publisher, but it would be highly unlikely to be one for a relatively large publisher. Consequently, a book that does not appear to have the potential to sell huge numbers of copies is more likely to be marketed aggressively by a relatively small than by a relatively large publisher.

## Competition with Similar Publications in House

Some publishers will publish more than one book for a particular market (audience). A large college textbook publisher, for example, might publish more than one book for a particular course. If a publisher already has a book in print that would compete directly with yours, you might not want to have that firm publish yours because you would have to compete for marketing resources. Of course, if your book is regarded as having greater sales potential that the existing one, then having to compete with it in house for marketing resources might not be a problem.

## Royalties and Other Contract Terms

If an acquisitions editor likes your proposal, he or she is likely to offer you a publishing contract. A publisher's standard contract is written by its attorneys and is likely to be extremely biased in favor of the publisher. Your impulse will be to sign it immediately—before the acquisitions editor has an opportunity to change his or her mind. Do not do so. Acquisitions editors are thrilled when authors sign contracts as is, but they are almost always willing to negotiate some of the clauses, including those pertaining to royalty percentages and advances. For information about the clauses that you are likely to be able to negotiate and practical advice for negotiating them, see Chapter 5 in Silverman (1998a).

# 8

# Copyright and Fair Use

Congress shall have the power . . . to promote the progress of science and useful arts by securing for limited times for authors. . . the exclusive right to their . . . writings.
— Article 1, Section 8 of the Constitution of the United States

While you are functioning as a scholar, you create intellectual property and use that created by others. The framers of the Constitution of the United States felt that the need for authors to have the exclusive right to benefit from what they create was so important that they gave Congress the power to enact whatever laws were necessary to insure authors having it. Congress provided this protection for authors by passing copyright laws. These laws place restrictions and obligations on both your use of others' intellectual property and their use of yours. Your failure to comply with these restrictions and obligations can result in your being sued. Furthermore, your failure to be knowledgeable about them can result in your not benefiting fully from the protection that they provide. My primary objective in this chapter is to acquaint you with the aspects of copyright law that will enable you to both avoid being sued for inappropriately using the works of others and to document your ownership of the writings and other works that you author.

## OBJECTIVES OF COPYRIGHT LAW

A copyright is the right to copy an author's work. The person owning the copyright, who might be the author, has the exclusive right for a specified period of time to make and sell copies of the work; consequently, he or she holds the copyright for the work. The work might be perceivable by vision, audition, touch, or some combination of the three. Works of authorship that are perceivable by vision include books, electronic publications on the Internet, computer programs, photographs, and drawings. An example of a work of authorship that is perceivable by audition is a sound recording on an audiotape cassette, site on the World Wide Web, computer disk, phonograph record, compact disk, or digital audiotape cartridge. An example of a work of authorship that is perceivable by touch is a book printed in braille. Examples of works of authorship that are perceivable through more than one sense modality are videotape recordings, sound motion pictures, and computer multimedia presentations.

Copyright laws have two basic objectives, both of which can be inferred from Article 1, Section 8 of the Constitution (quoted earlier in this chapter). The first "is to foster the creation and dissemination of intellectual works for the public welfare" (Dible, 1978, p. 115). These laws give the person who publishes intellectual works for the public welfare (who might be their author) the opportunity to recoup expenses and possibly make a profit. They do this by making it unlawful for someone else to make copies of the work and sell them for the duration of its copyright. If there were no copyright laws, publishers would be hesitant to invest the money necessary to publish a work because someone else could make copies of the work and possibly sell them at a lower price. They might be able to sell them at a lower price because they would not have some of the production expenses of the original publisher such as copyediting and typesetting. (The assumption here is that they would copy the book photographically.)

The second objective of copyright laws "is to give the creators the *reward* due them for their contribution to society" (Dible, 1978, p. 115, italics added). They do this in two ways: first, by requiring anyone who copies part of an author's work to indicate the title of the work and the name of its author and, second, by protecting the author's right to profit financially (for example, by receiving royalties) from the sale of copies of his or her works. No one is permitted to make and sell copies of an author's work without permission for the duration of the copyright. Presumably, if an author gives someone permission to make and sell copies of a work that he or she created, the author will be paid a certain agreed to amount for the permission to do so (possibly as a royalty on each copy sold).

## PROVISIONS OF COPYRIGHT LAW

The regulations pertaining to copyrights in the United States are contained in the Copyright Act of 1976 (Public Law 94-553). This was the first general revision of U.S. copyright law since 1909. The act became fully effective on January 1, 1978.

The Copyright Act of 1976 is a complex statute. Because of space limitations, I cannot discuss all aspects (or even all major aspects) of it here. My presentation will be limited to aspects that are likely to be relevant to the activities of scholars. The order in which topics are discussed corresponds roughly to the order in which they are mentioned in the statute. (The primary source for this discussion was Dible, 1978, pp. 111–254.)

### Duration of Copyright Protection

For works of authorship created after January 1, 1978, the duration of copyright protection is the life of the author plus 50 years after his or her death. For works of more than one author, the 50-year period is measured from the date of the death of the last surviving author. All copyrights run through December 31 of the calendar year in which they expire.

### Material That Can Be Copyrighted

The 1976 Copyright Act substitutes "original works of authorship" for "writings of an author" when designating the material that can be copyrighted. Original works of authorship that can be copyrighted under this act are not limited to those containing written words (which are referred to in the statute as "literary works"). These also include pictorial, graphic, and sculptural works; motion pictures and other audiovisual works; sound recordings; and computer programs.

Literary works includes any works expressed in "words, numbers, or other verbal or numerical symbols or indicia." Although a literary work has to be original in the sense of not being merely a copy of a preexisting work, there is no requirement that it be novel, or ingenuous, or possess esthetic merit. Almost any diagnostic or progress report could be classified for purposes of copyright as a literary work.

Pictorial, graphic, and sculptural works include photographs and drawings (such as those used in diagnostic tests and kits of therapy materials). Photographs and drawings, like literary works, must be original in the sense of not being merely copies of preexisting images, but their novelty, ingenuity, and esthetic merit are not considerations in determining whether they can be copyrighted.

Motion pictures and other audiovisual works include videotapes; sound recordings include phonograph records, audiotapes, compact disks, and digital audiotape cartridges. Again, novelty, ingenuity, and esthetic merit are not considerations in determining whether a work can be copyrighted.

Computer programs include both the code of which programs are comprised and the audiovisual displays that the code produces. These may be copyrighted separately because substantially the same visual or audiovisual effect can be achieved by different sets of computer code (Chickering & Hartman, 1987). With computer programs (as with the other categories of material) novelty, ingenuity, or esthetic merit are not considerations in determining whether a work can be copyrighted.

Thus far in this section I have dealt with material that can be copyrighted. Six types of materials mentioned in the act are denied U.S. copyright protection. Two are likely to be of particular interest to scholars. The first of these is ideas, methods, systems, and principles. One of the fundamental principles promulgated by this act is that "copyright does not protect ideas, methods, systems, principles, etc. but rather the *particular manner* in which they are expressed or described" (Dible, 1978, p. 127, italics added). Consequently, a copyright does not protect a scholar's ideas or methods from being copied; it only protects the particular arrangement of words in which he or she expresses or describes them.

A second type of subject matter that is denied U.S. copyright protection and is of interest to scholars is works of the U.S. government. According to Dible (1978, p. 128), "works produced for the U.S. Government by its officers and employees *as a part of their official duties* are not subject to U.S. copyright protection" (italics added). This category does not necessarily include works prepared under a U.S. government contract or grant. The funding agency can decide whether an independent contractor or grantee will be allowed to copyright works that were supported wholly or partially by government funds.

## Ownership and Transfer of Rights

The author of a work that was not prepared within the scope of his or her employment is the owner of the copyright on it unless he or she has transferred ownership of the copyright to somebody else. If such a work has more than one author, its authors jointly own the copyright unless they have transferred ownership of the copyright to somebody else.

The copyright to a work prepared by an employee within the scope of his or her employment belongs to the employer unless the employer transfers it to the employee in writing. Such a work is referred to in the copyright act as a work made for hire. "The rationale for this rule is that the work is produced under the employer's direction and expense; also the employer bears the risks and should be allowed to reap the benefits" (Dible, 1978, p. 130). Your employer, however, would not be entitled to the copyright on a work you wrote that was not prepared within the scope of your employment. If you plan to write something from which you hope to profit financially; if you will be doing it wholly or partially on the job or at your employer's expense, your employer might feel that he or she will be entitled to ownership of the copyright on it. To avoid a misunderstanding after the work is completed, it probably would be a good idea before beginning it to request a letter from your employer acknowledging your right to copyright the work in your name (or if your employer contributes significantly to the creation of it, in both your names). Another way to avoid such a misunderstanding is to work on the project at home on your own time.

It is perhaps more important now than it was previously for you to determine your institution's policy regarding copyright ownership before writing a book or creating some other intellectual property that has the potential to produce income. Your institution's policy on copyright is usually spelled out in the patent and copyright policies section of its faculty handbook. Some colleges and universities have begun, as a condition of employment, to require faculty to turn over the rights to at least some of the intellectual property they create, even if they worked on it exclusively in their home, with their own equipment, and on their own time.

An author might wish to transfer his or her rights to a work to somebody else. The reason for this, in most cases, would be that the author expected to profit from doing so. A publisher, for example, might agree to pay the author a royalty on each copy of his work sold in exchange for this transfer of rights. An author can sometimes negotiate a contract that allows him or her to retain the copyright on a work and then only sell (usually through an agent) certain rights to publishers (for example, translation rights). By negotiating this type of contract the author is, in effect, transferring ownership of a part of the copyright.

### Reproduction of Copyrighted Materials and the Doctrine of Fair Use

The Copyright Act of 1976 places certain restrictions on prohibiting the reproduction of copyrighted materials. One such restriction has been referred to as the doctrine of fair use. For an in-depth discussion of this doctrine, see the Copyright Act and Dible (1978).

The doctrine of fair use, which was developed by the courts, "allows copying without permission from, or payment to, the copyright owner where the use is reasonable and not harmful to the rights of the copyright owner" (Dible, 1978, p. 142). Without this doctrine, no use of copyrighted material would be possible without the copyright owner's permission. The idea here is that certain uses of copyrighted materials are not harmful to the rights of the copyright owner and promote the public welfare.

What can be copied under this doctrine? The excerpt from Section 107 of the Act, reproduced below, though somewhat vague, provides some general guidelines:

The fair use of a copyrighted work, including such use by reproduction in copies or phonograph records or by other means . . . for purposes such as criticism, comment, news reporting, teaching (including multiple copies for classroom use), scholarship, or research, is not an infringement of copyright. In determining whether the use made of a work in any particular case is a fair use the factors to be considered shall include—

(1) the purpose and character of the use, including whether such use is of a commercial nature or is for nonprofit educational purposes;

(2) the nature of the copyrighted work;

(3) the amount and substantiality of the portion used in relation to the copyrighted work as a whole; and

(4) the effect of the use upon the potential market for or value of the copyrighted work.

With regard to the first of these guidelines, the courts tend to look upon journal articles and academic books (with the possible exception of highly profitable ones used as texts for introductory courses) as being closer to the nonprofit educational end of the commercial continuum than to the trade book end of it. Consequently, they tend to define fair use for them fairly liberally.

With regard to the second, the courts tend to define fair use fairly conservatively for copyrighted works that are not professional or academic books or journals. Consequently, it is probably a good idea to get written permission before quoting even a few lines of text from a publication that is not a professional or academic one.

The third of these is one of the two most important determiners of whether a court is likely to look upon this doctrine as being applicable. Quoting more than a line or two from a very short work (for example, a poem) definitely requires written permission. Although there is not general agreement among specialists on copyright law on the amount it is safe to quote from an article in a professional journal or from a professional or academic book without written permission, most would agree that up to 250 words is permissible, providing the quote is indicated as such and is appropriately referenced.

The final guideline—the impact that the use is likely to have on sales of the work—is the other important determiner of the applicability of this doctrine. The situation in which it can be applied with most confidence is one in which it would be farfetched for a copyright owner to claim that the use adversely affected sales or would be likely to do so. A court would almost always regard it as being farfetched for the publisher of a professional or scientific journal to claim that quoting fewer than 200 words from an article reduced sales of the journal.

In addition to these guidelines for applying the fair use doctrine, specific ones have been developed for teaching. These guidelines permit teachers to make single copies of copyrighted materials for use in their teaching. They also permit teachers to make multiple copies for classroom use if the number of copies does not exceed the number of pupils in the class and the following restrictions are adhered to:

(1)  the copies may not be used as a substitute for anthologies, compilations, or collective works;

(2)  copies cannot be made of consumable materials such as work books;

(3)  the copies cannot be a substitute for purchases, be "directed by higher authority," or be repeated by the same teacher from term to term; and

(4)  there is no charge to the student beyond the actual copying cost. (Dible, 1978, p. 143)

There is a specimen letter for requesting permission to reproduce copyrighted material in Silverman (1998a). For further information about fair use and copyright, see Blue (1990), Bunnin and Beren (1988), Jassin and Schechter (1998), Kozak (1990), Luey (1987), Novick and Chasen (1984), and Strong (1984).

### Notice of Copyright

A copyright notice should be placed on all works for which copyright protection is desired. On visually perceptible copies, the notice should contain the following three elements:

(1) the symbol © (the letter C in a circle), or the word Copyright, or the abbreviation Copr.;

(2) the year of the first publication of the work; and

(3) the name of the owner of the copyright in the work, or an abbreviation by which the name can be recognized, or a generally known designation of the owner. (Dible, 1978, pp. 228–29)

However, "subject to certain safeguards for innocent infringers, protection would not be lost by the complete omission of the notice from large numbers of copies or from a whole edition, if registration of the work is made before or within *five years after publication*" (Dible, 1978, p. 165, italics added). Consequently, immediate, formal application for a copyright is not a prerequisite for placing a copyright notice on a work or for securing copyright protection for it. The mere placement of a copyright notice on a work ordinarily is sufficient to discourage persons from copying it without permission. The formal registration of a copyright, however, does increase the number of remedies that its owner can seek from a court.

### Deposit and Registration of Work to be Copyrighted

The formal copyrighting of a work ordinarily involves depositing two complete copies in the Library of Congress and completing an application for copyright registration and paying the required fee. (For an in-depth description of the application procedure, see Chickering & Hartman, 1987.) Depositing the two copies of the work in the Library of Congress is not always a prerequisite for securing copyright protection. It would not be one if fewer than five copies of the work have been published or the work is an expensive limited edition with numbered copies for which the requirement to deposit two copies would be burdensome, unfair, or unreasonable (see Section 407C of the 1976 Copyright Act). A multimedia project that a scholar self-publishes in a limited edition might be exempt from the deposit requirement.

## Copyright Infringement and Remedies

Owners of a copyright can seek several types of remedies from a court if the copyright is infringed. They can ask the court to issue an injunction or restraining order that will temporarily or permanently prevent or stop infringements. They can ask the court to impound all allegedly infringing copies of the work during the time a suit for infringement is pending. They can ask the court to award compensatory damages, which would offset the profits they lost because of the sale of the infringer's copies, or they can ask the court to award them statutory damages, which are a type of punitive damages that defendants can be required to pay simply because they infringed the plaintiff's copyright. They are referred to as statutory damages because they are specified in the statute or law.

# 9

# Ethical Issues

Rather than moralize, let me remind you very simply that you have an obligation to credit others accurately and fully for their work. "Others" include colleagues whose work you have used, students who have assisted with research, and friends or informants who have provided information. "Work" includes words, ideas, drawings, memories, data — all the raw material of scholarship. All original work is built upon the contributions of others and these contributions must be acknowledged. I must remind you also that what you write should be true — no falsified data, no fictional notes, no creative quotations.

— Luey, 1987, p. 73

To both receive and retain tenure, how you function as a scholar must be viewed by your colleagues as being ethical. Although the members of a tenure committee might be willing to forgive a publication record that is not exemplary, they are highly unlikely to forgive plagiarism or any other *clear-cut* breach of academic ethics. The word "clear-cut" was italicized because the decision whether an action is unethical is often a difficult one to make.

There can be several reasons for a lack of consensus about whether a particular action by a scholar is ethical. One relates to the fact that ethical judgments are based on what is known as natural law. According to the natural law philosophy, people are obliged to do what is good and avoid doing what is bad. Unfortunately, there is far from universal agreement about whether certain actions are good or bad. Contemporary examples include abortion, cloning, and assisted suicide.

Another reason that there is a lack of consensus about whether a particular action by a scholar is ethical is the existence of incompatible ethical obligations. If you behave ethically with regard to one you will behave unethically with regard to the other (or others). A speech-language pathologist who is employed in the public schools, for example, is required by her profession's code of ethics to both furnish the most appropriate diagnostic label for a child's disorder and hold paramount the welfare of persons served professionally. If she felt that a child would be likely to benefit from services that she could provide, but the most appropriate diagnostic label would not permit her to add the child to her caseload (because it is not a diagnosis for which funding is provided), she might decide to furnish a less appropriate diagnostic label that would enable the child to be added. Consequently, she would be considering the ethical obligation to hold paramount the child's welfare to be more important than that to furnish the most appropriate diagnostic label for his or her disorder.

The ethical issues dealt with in this chapter are not the only ones with which academic authors have to cope, and the order in which they are discussed is not intended to suggest their importance. Your failure to be sensitive to these issues, however, could impede your getting tenure and retaining it. For others, see the section in your faculty handbook dealing with your institution's policy on ethical conduct in research.

## HONESTY IN GATHERING, REPORTING, AND INTERPRETING DATA

Scholars must be able to trust each other's reports because they are unlikely to have the time and resources to independently verify the accuracy of all of the information in them that they use in their own research and writing. I will discuss the types of information in reports that scholars must be able to accept on faith as being accurate and complete.

### Review of the Literature

Reviews of the literature must be both accurate and complete. Your comments about findings and interpretations must be accurate. You must not modify the material you quote in a way that changes its meaning. You should not ignore literature that does not support your positions. At the very least, you should acknowledge that not all scholars agree with them and cite a few papers or books from which readers can learn about alternative viewpoints. Your failure to do so could be interpreted as a lack of familiarity with the literature which, of course, would not tend to enhance your reputation as a scholar.

## Scientific Justification

You should not suggest that you are the first to attempt to answer a question, test a hypothesis, or integrate the findings of the research on a problem if you are not the first to do so. You should acknowledge previous attempts and indicate why another (that is, yours) is necessary.

## Description of What Was Observed

You should describe the relevant attributes of the subjects or events you observed as accurately and completely as you can. It is particularly important that you indicate anything about them that could affect the ability to make generalizations from your findings.

## Description of How the Observations Were Made

You should describe the methodology that you used for making observations as accurately and completely as you can. Ways in which your methodology could have affected what you observed should be indicated. Furthermore, you should provide information about the validity and reliability of observations yielded by your methodology. This information could be from data you collected or the literature.

## Description of How the Data Were Analyzed

Anything about your data analyses that could have biased your outcomes should be indicated. Some possibilities are:

your elimination of data from subjects who did not appear to follow instructions;

your choice of a significance test, or tests;

your choice of a level of confidence for running significance tests;

assumptions not being met that could affect the interpretation of significance test results (for example, your subjects not being selected randomly from the population to which generalizations are made); or the likelihood that failure to reject a null hypothesis resulted from a Type II error. (see Chapter 10 in Silverman, 1998b)

### Data Reported

You should report your data accurately and in ways that are unlikely to cause them to be interpreted inappropriately. Graphs, for example, should not be plotted so that relatively small differences appear to be relatively large ones.

### Interpretation of the Data

You should indicate the amount of confidence that readers can have in each of your interpretations. Some of your interpretations might be ones with which almost all scholars in your field would agree and others might be speculations. Although it is certainly acceptable to speculate, you should indicate that you are speculating when doing so.

## PLAGIARISM

Intentional plagiarism almost universally is regarded as being a sufficient reason for denying tenure. It also can be a legally justifiable reason for taking tenure away.

You plagiarize when you attempt to pass off the words or ideas of somebody else as your own. You communicate them orally or in writing without acknowledging their source. You, however, might not be consciously aware that they are somebody else's words or ideas. Few of us have escaped the embarrassing experience of discovering that some words or ideas we thought were ours originated elsewhere.

Although you certainly should attempt to avoid any form of plagiarism, the type that is most likely to cause you problems with tenure is intentional plagiarism. This is where you consciously attempt to pass off the words or ideas of somebody else as your own. An example would be submitting a manuscript to a journal that was written by somebody else (for example, a graduate student) but that had only your name on the title page.

Unfortunately, it is practically impossible to always be aware that you are expressing the words or ideas of others when doing so. This is particularly true for ideas. The seeds for many, perhaps most, of the ideas that we write and talk about come from conversations we have had with others and things we have read that were written by others. We cannot acknowledge those who planted them because we cannot remember who they are. Perhaps the most honest thing to do, particularly in a book, is to acknowledge that the seeds for the ideas presented were planted over a number of years through conversations with students and colleagues and through reading.

Plagiarism can result in copyright infringement. You infringe a person's copyright by publishing his or her words without acknowledging their source. Doing the same for someone's ideas does not result in copyright infringement because ideas cannot be copyrighted (see Chapter 8).

## DESIGNATING AUTHORSHIP

The persons who are listed as coauthors of a publication should be those who made a significant contribution to creating it. It is questionable ethically to allow yourself to be listed as a coauthor of a paper to which you did not make a significant contribution. The types of contributions you could make include:

generating the concept or outline for the paper,

drafting the manuscript,

supervising (directing) at least some of the research reported in the paper, or

conducting at least some of the research reported in the paper.

In contrast, the types of contributions you could make to a paper that most scholars would not consider sufficient to ethically justify your being designated a coauthor (but would certainly warrant your being acknowledged) include:

funding the research reported in the paper;

providing equipment or facilities for the research reported in the paper;

being an administrator of an institution in which the research was conducted; and

running subjects, analyzing data, and doing other research-related tasks in which you are merely following orders (i.e., functioning as a research assistant).

Some scholars would, under certain circumstances, accept it as justifiable to list someone as a coauthor for making one or more of the contributions indicated above. They would be particularly likely to do so for a project that could not be completed otherwise and the price asked is inclusion as a coauthor.

It can be harmful to include articles in your application for tenure for which you cannot prove that you contribution was sufficient to warrant your being designated a coauthor. Members of your tenure committee are very likely to question your contribution to the articles you list of which you were not the first or second author, particularly if there are several such articles. You might want to include a statement in the application about your contribution to each of them.

## REVIEWING FOR JOURNALS AND CONFERENCES

One indicator that you are beginning to establish a reputation as a scholar is to be asked to review papers for journals or conferences. Your ability to not only do so well, but ethically, can significantly affect your reputation as a scholar and, consequently, your prospects for promotion and tenure. A number of these ethical considerations are discussed.

### Conflict of Interest

Conflict of interest could occur if you were doing research on the same problem or were writing (or planning to write) a paper on the same topic. You might consciously or unconsciously have a mind set to find a reason to reject the paper or, if it is being considered for publication in a journal, to delay reviewing it sufficiently long to complete your project and submit it for publication. If there is any possibility of there being a conflict of interest, you should return the paper to the editor with a note indicating why you are doing so. Returning it is not only desirable because it is the ethical thing to do, it also is desirable because it is likely to enhance your reputation as a scholar.

### Confidentiality

It is unethical to communicate any of the content of the papers you review to others without their authors' permission. It is also unethical to communicate the content of a review to anyone except the editor who commissions it or the editor's assistant.

### Using Some of the Ideas or Material in Your Research

It would certainly be regarded as unethical for you to plagiarize material from manuscripts that you are asked to review. It also could be regarded as unethical for you to use research ideas from the manuscripts you review that are rejected. The ethics here is not clear-cut. Although, on the one hand, you are plagiarizing an idea, on the other hand, you might be doing research that is likely to significantly benefit society and unlikely to be done otherwise.

### Attacking Authors Personally

It is absolutely unacceptable to attack an author personally in a review of his or her manuscript. You can do a candid review of a manuscript — even one that is highly critical — without berating its author or authors. Perhaps the main reason why you should avoid including personal attacks in your reviews is that including them can damage your reputation. Although people might enjoy reading exposés of celebrities in supermarket tabloids, they are unlikely to respect the tabloids for publishing them. Similarly, although colleagues can enjoy reading insulting reviews of manuscripts, they are highly unlikely to respect the person who wrote them. Furthermore, editors are unlikely to retain referees who write such reviews. While I was an associate editor of my association's research journal, one review of this type was sufficient to justify having someone removed from the editorial board.

## PROTECTION OF SUBJECTS

You have an ethical (as well as a legal) obligation to protect persons who serve as subjects from being harmed. For the past 50 years, the National Institutes of Health and other agencies — both here and abroad — have been promulgating guidelines and requirements that are intended to protect them. There is, in fact, likely to be a committee at your college or university that must approve research proposals in which human subjects are used before the research is begun and the proposal is submitted. Failing to conform to these guidelines and requirements is highly unlikely to enhance your prospects for getting tenure.

## USING DATA ABOUT ABUSED SUBJECTS

Is it ethical to use research data from abused subjects, particularly knowingly abused subjects? An extreme example of such data would be that from medical experiments on Jews and others in concentration camps by Nazi Germany during World War II. Each of us, of course, must answer this question for our self. The following is a comment by Dr.

Tomas Radil-Weiss, a psychiatrist, who was imprisoned at Auschwitz Concentration Camp when he was 14 years old.

The second world war ended many years ago. Most of those who survived the stay at the German concentration camp at Auschwitz have already died of the consequences of their imprisonment; those still alive are already in the last third of their life. Is there any point to returning to the experiences of those days? Consideration of the mental hygiene of former prisoners cautions us that perhaps we should not do it. *But consideration of the general interest holds that we are not entitled to ignore any knowledge that can contribute to social development — including medicine and psychology — even if acquired under unspeakably awful conditions.* (Radil-Weiss, 1983, p. 259, italics added)

Perhaps the use of such data can allow a little good to come from the suffering of research subjects who have been abused physically or psychologically, purposefully or through negligence.

# 10

## Preparing the Publication Section of a Promotion and Tenure Application

A semantic reaction is the psycho-logical reaction of a given individual to words and language and other symbols and events in connection with their meanings.

— Korzybski, 1958, p. 24

You, of course, want the persons who evaluate your application for tenure to react favorably to the publication section — that is, have a positive semantic reaction to it. Their reaction to your publication record will be determined by the meaning — both intellectual and emotional — that it has for them. We will explore some strategies in this chapter by which you may be able to increase the likelihood that their semantic reaction to your publication record will be a positive one.

### SEMANTIC REACTIONS

We react to stimuli based on the meanings that they have for us. Korzybski (1958) chose the term "semantic" to label this type of reaction because of the term's association with meaning (that is, linguistic meaning). He was one of the first (in the early 1930s) to point out that all stimuli — not just words — have meaning. The meaning of a stimulus to an observer almost always has both emotional and intellectual aspects. The emotional aspects can be a more important determiner of an observer's reactions to a stimulus than the intellectual ones, but he or she might not be conscious of it being so. Because observers' reactions to stimuli are determined by the meanings that they have for them, how a stimulus is presented can influence the meaning and, consequently, their reaction to it. Politicians, for example, are aware of this and employ spin doctors to influence the meaning that they have (as a stimulus) for their constituents.

The stimulus to which the persons who read the publication section of your application for tenure will react consists of the pages on which it is printed. Although the words on these pages are certainly important determiners of their semantic reaction to this section, they are not the only determiners. This is particularly likely to be true if your publication record is not exemplary — for example, a dozen publications in prestige journals of which you are either the only author or the first coauthor. Some other factors that could influence their reaction to this part of your tenure application are indicated in the next section along with suggestions for coping with them.

## FACTORS THAT CAN INFLUENCE THE SEMANTIC REACTION TO THE PUBLICATION SECTION OF A TENURE APPLICATION

There are a number of factors that can influence the semantic reaction to the publication section of your tenure application.

### How Your Publications Are Organized

Journal and newsletter articles that have not been peer reviewed should be listed separately from those that have been peer reviewed. It is risky to combine the two because, if a member of your committee spots an article in the list that is not in a peer-reviewed journal, he or she may question whether the other articles in the list were peer reviewed. Most members of your institution's promotion and tenure committee will be from fields that do not publish in the same journals you do. Consequently, they are unlikely to be aware of which journals in your field do and do not routinely peer review articles.

Articles should be arranged by year of publication. Those in press and in submission should also be listed.

Books published, in press, and in process should be listed separately from journal articles. You might want to add information about reviews, translations, rights purchases by professional book clubs, awards, and adoptions (for textbooks) to the listings for books that have already been published.

You should also list chapters in books separately from journal articles. These are usually written by invitation and persons invited to write them tend to be ones who have at least begun to develop a national reputation. They might not, however, be peer reviewed before acceptance for publication as rigorously as journal articles. Consequently, it might be worthwhile to arrange to have them peer reviewed after they are published and include the reviews as an appendix to the application.

Papers presented at national or international conventions and conferences should also be listed. If you have given a number of such presentations, you might not want to bother listing local ones. Although presentations at national and international meetings are almost always regarded as evidence that a scholar has at least begun to develop a national or international reputation in his or her field, those at local meetings might not. In my experience, persons who include a long list of local presentations in their tenure application tend to be ones who have relatively weak publication records. It probably would be a good idea to have your convention and conference papers peer reviewed and include the reviews as an appendix to the application.

Other types of publications — including ones on audiotape, videotape, and computer disk — should also be listed separately. If they were not rigorously peer reviewed before publication, you should arrange to have this done and include the reviews as an appendix to the application.

You also might want to list editorships and publications and agencies for which you have peer-reviewed articles and grants in this section. It is worthwhile to mention them in this section because they are evidence that you have begun to develop a national reputation as a scholar.

## Credibility of Reviewers Used for Non–Peer-Reviewed Publications

It is crucial that the persons who do the reviewing are regarded as credible by the members of your promotion and tenure committee. Committee members most likely will assume that articles published in peer-reviewed journals are of adequate quality, whereas they might question the quality of those published in non–peer-reviewed journals. Consequently, you will have to assume the burden of proof that such publications are of adequate quality. The credibility of those who do the reviewing will certainly influence (perhaps determine) how successful you will be in doing so. For this reason, you should include sufficient information about the reviewers in the application to establish their credibility for reviewing the publications.

### Adequately Documenting Attempts to Secure Extramural Funding

When making tenure decisions some institutions give more weight to publications relating to projects for which extramural funding was secured. There are at least two reasons. First, the project reported in them had to survive a rigorous peer-review process to be funded. Second, the project could have generated substantial overhead income for the institution. Few colleges and universities would want to fire (deny tenure to) someone who has been and is likely to continue generating such income.

If there are projects for which you attempted to secure extramural funding but were not successful, you might want to document this in your application. You should certainly do so for any that were approved for funding but not funded because they were not high enough on the list. The fact that they were approved for funding is evidence that they were of sufficiently high quality to survive a rigorous peer-review process.

### Whether Your Publication Record Appears Padded

Most scholars occasionally give presentations about their research to students and faculty at their institution and others. They also might give presentations about their research to local professional or scientific groups or contribute articles about it to their newsletters. Although it is certainly desirable for an academic to share his or her knowledge in these ways, listing them in the scholarly activity section of a promotion and tenure application is more likely to harmful than helpful. At least a few members of your promotion and tenure committee are likely to assume that you included them in order to make your contribution to scholarship in your field appear more impressive than it really is. It would, however, be appropriate to mention them in the section of the application in which you are asked to document your service to your institution and community.

### Adequately Describing Your Contributions to Coauthored Publications

The members of your promotion and tenure committee are likely to question your contribution to publications you coauthored, particularly those for which you are not the first author. Consequently, you might want to be proactive and include a statement detailing your contributions to each coauthored publication.

## Adequately Documenting that Your Publications Appear in Respectable, Peer-Reviewed Journals

Few, if any, of the members of your promotion and tenure committee are likely to be familiar with all of the journals in which you published. If they are prestigious ones (for example, ones published by your professional association that have low acceptance rates), you might want to include some documentation for their being so.

## Adequately Documenting Commencement of a Program of Research

At least some of the members of your promotion and tenure committee are likely to scrutinize your publication record to determine if it has a focus. The persons from your field who are invited to evaluate your publication record are likely to do so also. The question they will attempt to answer is: Do the candidate's publications appear to be mainly opportunistic rather than suggesting an attempt (or attempts) to begin a systematic program of research? Opportunistic publications include ones that you wrote with others — usually not as first author — and the topics for which are neither your idea nor within your specialty. They are particularly likely in this regard to scrutinize your publications with graduate students. If most of your publications are coauthored by graduate students and they deal with topics that are not clearly related to your program of research, at least a few members of your promotion and tenure committee are likely to conclude that they were opportunistic. Although you certainly will get some credit for publications that are regarded as being opportunistic, you are likely to get more credit for ones that suggest you have been attempting to develop a program of research.

If it is not obvious how your coauthored publications — particularly those with graduate students — relate to your program of research, you might want to include a statement in your application detailing how they do so.

## How Strongly Your Publication Record Suggests that You Will Be a Productive Scholar If Tenured

One question that is almost certain to be raised during deliberations on your application is how likely you are to continue being productive as a scholar if tenured. The members of your committee are likely to assume that:

Persons who published regularly throughout their probationary period are more likely to continue being productive after they are tenured than those who published mostly at the end.

Persons who pursued a systematic program of research during their probationary period are more likely to continue being productive after they are tenured than those whose publications during this period were mainly opportunistic ones.

Persons who have more than the minimum number of publications that their department or college requires are more likely to continue being productive after they are tenured than those who merely have the minimum.

Persons who have begun to be recognized nationally as scholars during their probationary period are more likely than otherwise to continue being productive as scholars after they are tenured. Evidence of such recognition would include being asked to referee manuscripts for journals, being awarded research grants, being invited to participate in conferences, and being asked to contribute chapters to books.

If your publication record is not consistent with one or more of these assumptions, and you can explain why you are likely to continue being productive as a scholar if tenured in spite of it, without sounding defensive, you might want to consider doing so in the application.

### Adequately Documenting Development of a National Reputation as a Scholar

One question that is likely to be asked during a promotion and tenure deliberation is: Can we do better. At colleges and universities that expect their tenured faculty to be productive scholars, the deliberation is likely to focus on the likelihood that the person will become (or will continue being) a nationally prominent scholar. The institution is unlikely to want to grant tenure to someone who does not have this potential. One reason is that if they replace him or her with a new person with a doctoral degree, the institution can both save money on salary and possibly gain someone who does have the potential to develop a national reputation as a scholar. Consequently, it is crucial that you build the strongest case in your application that you can for your having begun to develop such a reputation. You can use any of the following as evidence for your having begun to do so:

citations of your publications by other scholars;

being asked to review academic book proposals; manuscripts submitted to scholarly, professional, or scientific journals; or research grant applications;

being invited to participate in academic conferences and convention sessions, possibly as a discussant;

being invited to write a chapter on your specialty for a book or a paper for a journal;

having your research funded by an agency of the federal government or a national foundation;

being interviewed by national media on a topic related to your specialty;

receiving an award for a publication or convention presentation;

being asked to serve as an expert witness on a topic related to your specialty;

being asked to serve on national committees related to your specialty, particularly ones that deal with scholarly activities (for example, your association's publication board); or

unsolicited fan mail from a well-known scholar about a research contribution.

There, of course, also can be other types of evidence that you could use to document that you have begun to develop a national reputation as a scholar.

### Credibility of the Scholars Who Evaluated Your Publications

If you or your department chairperson selects outside persons to evaluate your publication record, it is desirable that sufficient information about them be included in the application to establish their credibility. Although they may be well known and highly respected by scholars in your field, those outside of it are unlikely to be familiar with them.

## A FINAL COMMENT

If you keep the publication section of your promotion and tenure application in mind right from the beginning of your probationary period, your publication record is more likely to be adequate than if you only begin thinking about it near the end.

# 11

# Funding Research and Publication

The average applicant to NSF has the proposal funded on the third try. The statistics are similar for the other agencies. Although programs vary in their level of competitiveness. . . , all receive more good proposals than they can fund. If your proposal is rejected the first time, the best advice is to swallow hard, sleep on it, and persist.
                                                    — Knight, 1988, p. 185

To win at the publishing for tenure (PFT) game, you also might have to win at the extramural funding game. In some departments, winning at the extramural funding game is a means to an end and, in others, it is an end in itself. By it being an end in itself I mean that a faculty member who does not receive a significant amount of extramural grant funding is unlikely to receive tenure regardless of the number of publications that he or she has. Receiving extramural grant funding is more likely to be a requirement for tenure in science departments than in humanities departments.

It is extremely important to find out your department's policy regarding extramural funding and tenure at the beginning of your probationary period. Do the tenured faculty in your department consider receiving extramural funding to be an end in itself or merely something that could be necessary to facilitate your scholarly activities? The answer to this question will determine how you will have to play the PFT game to win. If receiving extramural funding is a requirement of being tenured, then you will have to pursue research that stands a chance of being fundable (regardless of whether it is research you would otherwise be interested in doing) and spend a great deal of time writing grant applications and revising rejected ones for resubmission.

Being required to get extramural funding to be supported for tenure might not be an official departmental policy. Rather, it could be a gentlemen's agreement among its tenured faculty. If it is not official policy, you will probably learn about it through the grapevine. It is, incidentally, something that you might want to tactfully inquire about when interviewing for a faculty position.

Why might a department be highly motivated to have a faculty member receive extramural funding? A department can benefit from such funding in many ways, some of which are indirect. They include:

The department is no longer obliged to fund the faculty member's scholarly activities from its budget. It is even relieved from having to fund from its budget such routine office expenses as the faculty member's postage, long distance telephone calls, and photocopying.

The department no longer has to fund a faculty member's entire salary from its budget. A quarter of it or more is likely to be funded by soft money from the grant. This provides the faculty member with released time from teaching to devote to research. Incidentally, at least some of the money that would have gone to the faculty member can remain in the departmental budget for discretionary use.

The department would receive funds that could be used to support graduate students and postdoctoral fellows, thereby attracting higher quality ones than it probably would be able to otherwise.

The department would receive funding that could be used to hire doctoral level research associates and other support personnel.

The department's status within its college or university would increase. One reason is that a college or university could receive some funds from a faculty member's grant to support administering it.

The status of the department within its field would increase. Extramural funding of faculty research is one of the factors that is usually considered when rating (ranking) departments nationally.

The receipt of the funding facilitates the faculty member's ability to both publish sufficiently to be tenured and begin developing a national reputation as a scholar.

There undoubtedly are ways in addition to these that a department could benefit from its faculty receiving extramural funding.

My primary focus in this chapter will be on PFT in departments where grants are regarded as means to ends rather than ends in themselves. If you are in a department in which you must receive extramural funding to receive tenure, then you will have to focus on securing such funding right from the beginning of your probationary period. Unfortunately (as the quotation at the beginning of this chapter suggests), doing so is unlikely to be easy.

## DEPENDING ON EXTRAMURAL FUNDING FOR PUBLISHING FOR TENURE CAN BE RISKY

I have both good news and bad news if you are seeking extramural funding support for your scholarly activities. The good news is that hundreds of millions of dollars are awarded every year to support such activities. The bad news is that many more worthwhile proposals are submitted to most governmental- and private-funding entities than they can fund.

There are two generalizations about extramural funding that can make it risky to depend on it for developing an adequate PFT record:

Most extramural grant proposals — particularly ones submitted by investigators who do not have a substantial publication record — never get funded.

Extramural grant proposals that do get funded rarely do so the first time that they are submitted.

If most or all of the PFT that you are planning to do cannot be done without your applying for and receiving extramural funding, the probability is high (perhaps greater than 50 percent) that you will not be able to do it or have enough time to do it before having to go up for tenure. Even if a proposal does eventually get funded, it is likely to take at least two or three resubmissions. This means that you could be halfway or more through your probationary period before you would be able to begin the research. Consequently, it is unlikely that you would be able to begin publishing your findings until the last year or two of your probationary period. You would be wise, therefore, to not put all of your eggs in one basket — that is, to also do projects that do not require extramural funding to complete and publish. Some possibilities for such projects are suggested elsewhere in the chapter.

## SOURCES OF FUNDING FOR
## RESEARCH AND PUBLICATION

There are many sources from which you might be able to get the funding you need to do a project. Some of them are discussed here.

### The Institution Where You Are Employed

This is the source from which you are most likely to be successful in getting funding for your research, particularly at the beginning of your probationary period. The grants they offer tend to be relatively small. Most are intended to provide seed money for getting a research project off the ground. The institution can require that recipients seek or have sought extramural funding for their projects. A requirement for a summer faculty fellowship at my university, for example, is to have sought extramural funding for the project being proposed.

### Federal, State, and Local Government Agencies

Such agencies historically have been major funding sources for academic research in all fields. Most federal agencies and some state and local ones have grant programs, including ones for scholars early in their careers. The office for research support at your institution is likely to be your best source for up-to-date information about these programs. It also can provide the help you need to prepare a proposal that stands a chance of being funded for submission to a government agency.

Some government agencies issue research requests for proposals. The agency defines the research it wants done and invites persons to submit proposals for doing it. If you receive the contract for doing the project, you might not be allowed to publish the findings. This would not necessarily diminish the value of such a project for enhancing your reputation as a scholar and getting tenure. Others who competed would probably be informed (directly or indirectly) that you received the contract, which would tend to enhance your reputation as a scholar, at least a little. The upper administration of your institution also would be aware that you received it, which is likely to motivate them to want to keep you. The office for research support at your institution might be willing to alert you to requests for proposals that could be relevant to your research interests.

## Private Nonprofit Agencies and Foundations

Thousands of private nonprofit agencies and foundations have funded academic research. They are of two types. The first consists of nonprofit agencies and foundations that have sharply focused program interests. They include disability-related associations (for example, the Muscular Dystrophy Association), religious organizations, political organizations, trade associations, special-interest (lobbying) groups, and family-run philanthropies. Because awarding grants is not their primary mission, their grant programs tend to be relatively small and operate informally without full-time professional staff.

The second type consists of broad-based philanthropic foundations (for example, the Ford Foundation) that conduct regular, ongoing grant programs. There are fewer of them than of the first type. Because their primary mission is to award grants, their resources tend to be large and they operate formally with a full-time professional staff.

There are resources available for identifying nonprofit agencies and foundations that might be interested in a project for which you are seeking funding. You should contact your institution's office that deals with foundation support before doing a search or contacting foundations for two reasons. First, this office can help you to identify foundations that are likely to be interested in your project and to contact them. Second, it can prevent you from getting into trouble with your institution by approaching a foundation from which it is currently seeking, or is planning to seek, a large grant. A foundation that awards a small grant to you might be less likely to award your institution the large one it is seeking.

## Individuals

Although it is rather unusual for a research project or program to be funded by an individual, it might be a possibility worth exploring. The donor would make a tax-deductible gift to your college or university that was restricted to supporting your research. The gift might not be a one-time one and could include, or consist of, a bequest. The gift could serve as a memorial for someone (for example, a spouse or child who died of a disease for which you are trying to find a cure). One way that you might be able to locate such a person is to publicize your research program in your local print and electronic media and indicate that you are seeking this type of support.

### Corporations

The research grant programs sponsored by corporations usually are directly related to their products or services. Your findings could be regarded as proprietary and, consequently, you might not be allowed to publish them. This could limit their usefulness for developing both the type of publication record and national reputation needed to be tenured. In departments (such as engineering) that have a history of relying on corporate funding for research, your inability to publish your findings might not interfere with your being granted tenure. There are resources available that identify and describe some corporate research grant programs. Your institution's office of research support should be able to help you find those programs for which your project might be appropriate.

## FUNDING STRATEGIES

Most research grant programs receive more fundable proposals than they have the resources to fund. Consequently, they are likely to rank those they regard as fundable, based on a number of criteria, and fund from the top of the list down until the money runs out. Your goal, therefore, should be to write a proposal that the granting entity is likely to regard as fundable and for which they can develop sufficient enthusiasm to place it high on their list. Some of the things you can do to maximize your likelihood of achieving this goal are discussed here.

### Establish a Good Working Relationship with the Staff of Your Institution's Office of Research or Foundation Support

Establishing a good working relationship with such an office's staff can facilitate your getting a grant in at least two ways. First, it could cause them to take a personal interest in your project and, consequently, invest more of themselves than they would otherwise in helping you identify possible funding sources. Second, because they have invested themselves in identifying possible funding sources, they are likely to provide you with more assistance than otherwise when preparing grant applications and when revising them for resubmission if they are rejected.

## Submit Proposals to Entities that Have Recently Funded Similar Types of Projects

An excellent proposal is almost certain to be rejected if it is submitted to an entity that does not have as a part of its mission supporting the type of research being proposed. Most funding entities have a narrow focus of interest — sometimes very narrow — that is likely to change at least a little over time. One way to infer how likely an entity's staff is to regard your project as having the appropriate focus is determining whether any of the projects that it has funded recently have a focus similar to yours. Although your project might have the appropriate focus for last year's competition, there is no guarantee that it will for this year's, but the probability is high enough to warrant approaching the entity.

A year-by-year listing of grants that an entity has funded is likely to be available. The staff at your institution's research or foundation support office can help you locate listings for those entities whose funding history would make it more likely that they would consider your project to be consistent with their mission.

### Discuss Your Proposal

The mission of a grant-funding entity is likely to change from time to time, at least a little. Consequently, although your project might be appropriate for a particular entity's mission last year, there is no guarantee that it will be this year. It is important, therefore, to contact those entities for which your project appears to be appropriate before submitting a formal application to ascertain how likely their staffs are to consider funding it a priority. The best way is to visit their offices. If this is not possible, you might be able to get the information that you need to determine their enthusiasm by phone. A project about which the staff seems to be enthusiastic is more likely to be funded than one for which their interest seems lukewarm. Although the persons with whom you discuss a project might not be the ones who make funding decisions, they would be likely to communicate their enthusiasm for the project (or lack of it) to those who make these decisions.

### Follow Proposal Preparation Instructions

Evaluating grant proposals is a very time-consuming task. If an entity has received many more proposals than it can fund, one way to reduce the number to which it has to give serious consideration is to eliminate those that were not prepared according to instructions. Even a relatively minor deviation from instructions can result in a proposal not being given serious consideration. One common deviation is that the proposal is longer than the maximum length specified in the instructions. Another deviation is that the sections in the proposal narrative are not presented in the order or format specified in the instructions.

## Answer All Questions

It will be necessary to generate some enthusiasm for your project to maximize the probability that, if it is approved for funding, it will be placed high enough on the list to be funded. Not all proposals that are approved for funding are funded. Available resources might be adequate to fund only a relatively small percentage of those that the review panel approves for funding. The level of enthusiasm that reviewers have for a proposal will influence the ratings they give it. Their ratings will be influenced by how convincingly you have established that there is a strong scientific justification for the project — that is, how well you have documented the importance of the project through your answers to the "so what" or "who cares" questions.

Perhaps the biggest mistake you can make here is assuming that the importance of the project is obvious. Because it seems obvious to you does not necessarily mean that it will be obvious to reviewers. You are more familiar with the literature and research needs in the area than at least some of them are likely to be. It is better to err by documenting its importance when doing so is not necessary than failing to do so when it is necessary.

## Document Your Ability to Complete the Project

Even if you are successful in convincing reviewers that the project you are proposing is important, they are unlikely to give your proposal a high rating unless they are convinced that you have the abilities and resources needed to do the project. Provide the strongest documentation that you can that you have these abilities and resources.

If this is your first grant and your publication record is not outstanding, it is likely to be difficult to convince reviewers that you can do the project unless the grant is either a relatively small one or one intended for beginning investigators. Perhaps the best way to convince reviewers that you can do the project is to collaborate on it with a senior faculty person who has a history of successfully completing projects for which he or she received extramural funding and, in addition, has a strong publication record.

## Present the Proposal in a Competent Manner

The appearance of a proposal — not just its content — tends to influence reviewers' judgments about its author's competence to do the project. Your proposals should be both well written and as attractive as you can make them without deviating from the agency's or foundation's guidelines. Your institution's office of research or foundation support should be able to assist you in organizing, writing, and formatting proposals so that they communicate competence.

## Revise and Resubmit Proposals

As the lines quoted at the beginning of this chapter suggest, a proposal is unlikely to be funded the first time that it is submitted. It is not unheard of for a proposal to have to be resubmitted four or five times before it is funded. Consequently, if you are going to be successful at grantsmanship, you are going to have to be both persistent and able to keep yourself from being demoralized by rejection.

## PRE–EXTRAMURAL FUNDING PUBLICATION

Even if you are successful in getting an extramural grant to fund your research, you are likely to be at least a year or so into your probationary period before you receive it. It is unwise to wait until you receive a grant to begin PFT. There are some types of projects that you might be able to do and publish without such funding, including:

Write a paper or two based on your dissertation data. Such a paper might not be one in which you use the data for the same purpose you did in your dissertation. That is, you might be able to use it to answer some other question or questions — perhaps ones that are more meaningful than those you used to answer in your dissertation. You also might be able to update your literature review and write a review paper.

Combine existing sets of published data that were intended to answer a particular question using meta-analysis (see Silverman, 1998b) or another statistical procedure. Few, if any, questions can be answered unequivocally with a single set of data. Many papers reporting this type of analysis have been published in at least a few fields, including psychology and medicine. Of course, if you have access to unpublished sets of data, they can be included also.

Collaborate with someone on a project who has a grant and can fund it. Ideally, the project should in the field in which you are attempting to establish a national reputation.

Apply for a small internal grant that will enable you to do a project that is likely to be publishable. The project could be justifiable as preliminary research for one for which you plan to seek extramural funding.

Undertake a publishable project that you can afford to fund yourself. It is likely to be cheaper to do this than to get a new job and move.

## MENTORING FOR GRANTSMANSHIP

You are unlikely to learn what you need to know to be successful at grantsmanship merely by reading books or attending seminars. You need to be coached by someone who has been successful at it. If you do not know such a person, your institution's office of research support might be willing to provide you with leads. Although it is desirable that the person is from your field, it is not essential. The rules for maximizing the likelihood of being successful are essentially the same for all fields.

Among the things that a mentor might be able to do for you are:

inform you about the rules by which the grantsmanship game is really played, which can differ significantly from those by which it is supposed to be played;

lend you research proposals that were funded to use as models;

critically review your proposals before they are submitted;

collaborate with you on a project; and

provide you with emotional support and encouragement, particularly after a proposal is rejected.

# 12

# Publishing with a Collaborator

To succeed as a collaborative writer, you need people skills in addition to writing skills. . . . You need to be able to get your ego out of
the way when conficts arise.
— Bennett & Larsen, 1988, p. 19

Many, perhaps most, academic books and journal articles are the product
of a collaboration. A collaborative publication can have more than one
author or its author(s) can acknowledge the assistance of one or more
persons. However, the fact that a publication involved some collaboration
is not always acknowledged (or acknowledged fully) in it. In some cases,
the withholding of such information is purposeful, thereby making it a
violation of scholarly ethics. In others, it merely reflects a lack of conscious
awareness of the impact that discussions with and comments by others
had in shaping the publication. One could argue, for example, that accepting suggestions from editors or reviewers makes them collaborators.

The focus of this chapter is on publishing with a coauthor. We will deal
with the potential benefits and losses from a coauthorship collaboration,
considerations when seeking a coauthor, and strategies you can use to
maximize the likelihood of a coauthorship collaboration being successful
— that is, the benefits to you outweigh the losses — including having a
joint collaboration agrccmcnt.

## POTENTIAL BENEFITS OF A COLLABORATION

There are many ways that you might be able to benefit from collaborating on an article, book, or other academic publication.

### Less Work

If you are a coauthor of a project and your coauthors do their fair share, then you will be required to do less work than you would if you did the project by yourself. However, if your coauthors do not do their fair share, you could end up spending more time than you would if you did the project yourself. The additional time would include that spent trying to motivate your coauthors to do what they promised.

### Feedback

Having to justify what you write is likely to reduce the number of positions you take that do not reflect sound scholarship. Also, having someone edit your writing is likely to improve it. Assuming that a coauthor is a good editor and as knowledgeable about the project as you, both of the above would tend to increase the likelihood that the project will be accepted for publication.

### Social Interaction

If you tend to avoid writing because it is a solitary activity, you could be more productive as a coauthor. Also, if you write projects with colleagues or friends, doing so can enhance your relationships with them assuming that things go well. If things do not go well, you could damage (perhaps even destroy) your relationship with them. Some things you can do to reduce the likelihood of damaging your relationships with coauthors are described elsewhere in the chapter.

### Expense Reduction

If you do not have a grant, you are likely to have to pay at least a few of the research and publication expenses for your projects out of pocket. (Your department's budget might cover some of them.) Publication expenses, for example, could include purchasing reprints and paying mandatory journal page charges. If a journal article or other publishing project you are doing has coauthors and if they are willing to share research and publication expenses with you, your costs will be reduced.

## Emotional Support

As I have indicated previously, rejections of journal articles, book proposals, and grant proposals are not uncommon. Such a rejection is a loss for which you will grieve. Having persons with whom you can share your grief is likely to provide emotional support that will help you to work your way through the grieving process (assuming, of course, that your coauthors do not become demoralized easily).

## Mentoring

An opportunity to write journal articles, books, or other publishing projects with a scholar who has been successful at doing the type of publishing you want to do can be a great learning experience. Perhaps the best way to learn how to win at the academic publishing game is to partner with someone who has a good win-loss record for the aspect of it that you are interested in. Even if the topic that the person is researching is not of particular interest to you, you can still learn quite a bit about playing the game by partnering with him or her.

## Enhancing Your Reputation by Linking Your Name with an Established Scholar

Writing journal articles or books with an established scholar in an area in which you are trying to establish a national reputation can help you to do so. It is particularly likely to help you establish a national reputation if you write a series of papers with that person. Be aware, however, that if most of your publications are of this type, your committee could question your ability to function independently as a scholar when you go up for tenure. At least a few members of your committee are likely to do so if most of your publications are written with your dissertation advisor or you are not first author on at least some of your coauthored publications. As I have indicated previously, it is important in your tenure application to document your contributions to coauthored publications of which you are not first author.

### Being Able to Take on a Project
### You Could Not Do Otherwise

You might lack the knowledge, skills, or resources needed to complete a publishing project, but by partnering with someone who has them, you might be able to publish a paper or book that you could not otherwise.

## POTENTIAL LOSSES FROM A COLLABORATION

Just as there are ways you can benefit by collaborating when publishing for tenure, there also are ways you can lose. You need to be aware of both to calculate a benefit to loss ratio for collaborating. We will discuss the ways that you can lose.

### Loss of Control

Collaboration almost always involves some loss of control. The amount of control that a person loses by collaborating is determined, at least in part, by his or her assertiveness and reputation as a scholar. The more assertive a person is and the greater the relative strength of his or her national reputation, the less control he or she is likely to lose by collaborating. A junior faculty member who collaborates with a senior faculty member — particularly one who has a strong national reputation as a scholar — is likely to experience considerable loss of control.

Regardless of your assertiveness or reputation as a scholar, by collaborating you relinquish the ability to make at least some decisions unilaterally. This can result in decisions that are compromises — ones with which you disagree. It can also result in your becoming frustrated because of the time it takes to make a decision. You are particularly likely to experience frustration for this reason if your status in the collaboration is relatively weak, and you are more motivated than the others to complete the project.

### Projects Take Longer to Complete

If a manuscript has more than one author, it might take longer to write than if it had a single author. There can be several reasons for this. One is the ability of its coauthors to make writing the manuscript a priority. The demands on their time may be such that they are unable to do so. Another is the time it takes to negotiate wordings — particularly wordings for conclusions. This time, of course, could be time well spent. That is, it could result in the manuscript being better written than it would have been otherwise, thereby increasing the likelihood of it being accepted for publication.

## Collaborators Do Not Always Fulfill Promises

If a person with whom you are collaborating does not do what he or she promised, the project might not be completed or completed on time. If, for example, a person who agreed to contribute a chapter to a book does not submit it by the date he or she promised, the publication of the book could be delayed or even canceled. All academic book-publishing contracts contain a clause that permits the publisher to refuse to publish a book if the manuscript is not submitted by the deadline indicated on the contract.

## Damaged or Destroyed Relationships

This is perhaps the most serious risk when writing a manuscript with a friend or colleague. The probability that your relationship with him or her will be damaged or destroyed is substantial, particularly if you did not negotiate a joint collaboration agreement before beginning the project. There are several issues that could result in hurt feelings if they are not resolved before the collaboration begins. One issue is whose name comes first in the listing of authors. This issue and some of the others that should be considered when negotiating a joint collaboration agreement are discussed elsewhere in this chapter.

## Disagreements about Interpretation of Data

Successful collaboration almost always involves compromise. One of the issues on which you might have to compromise in the write-up of a research study is how the data are interpreted. You and your coauthor (or coauthors) might not agree on the conclusions that it is reasonable to draw from them or their theoretical implications. This can leave you feeling less good about the article than you would have otherwise. Before agreeing to collaborate on a study, you might want to determine how your potential collaborators would interpret each of the possible outcomes.

## Less Ego Involvement and Sense of Ownership

You are likely to have less ego involvement with, and a weaker sense of ownership of, projects on which you collaborate. Although both can reduce the amount of satisfaction you get from having a manuscript accepted for publication, they can also reduce the amount of distress you experience from having one rejected.

### Reputation Establishment

Publications of which you are not first author are less likely than single-authored ones to help you establish a national reputation as a scholar. Such publications, however, can reinforce your national reputation if it is already established. Many established scholars, when they write papers with graduate students or junior faculty, list themselves second or third. Nevertheless, their name is the one that is most likely to be recognized and remembered.

### Copyright Ownership

The ownership of the copyright on a manuscript to which more than one author contributed might not be as clear-cut as that for a single-authored one. This is more likely to be worth worrying about for books and computer software than it is for journal articles. It can, for example, influence how royalty income is divided.

### Scholarly Independence

When you go up for tenure, if you have few single-authored publications or coauthored ones for which you are first author, your ability to function independently as a scholar is almost certain to be questioned. The best way to establish your ability to function independently as a scholar is by having a number of single-authored publications or coauthored ones for which you are first author.

## SEEKING A COAUTHOR

Unfortunately, there is no litmus test for predicting whether a collaboration will be successful. There are, however, some things you might want to consider when you seek a coauthor or decide whether to accept an invitation to be a coauthor that could influence the likelihood of your collaboration being successful.

### Comfort Level

If you cannot stand being with a person, you will probably want to avoid collaborating with him or her, even if the person would otherwise be an excellent collaborator. Such a person, for example, could be an ex-spouse.

## Dependability

If you do not know the person well enough to make this judgment, you could get the information you need from persons with whom he or she has collaborated previously. These do not have to be ones who did research with the person. They can be ones who served on a committee with him or her. You would be wise to avoid collaborating with someone who has a poor track record in this regard. Doing so can be extremely frustrating. Believing that the person has changed is likely to be wishful thinking.

## Enthusiasm

A person who is not enthusiastic about a project is unlikely to invest very much of himself or herself in it. Consequently, you would be wise to gauge a person's enthusiasm for a project before agreeing to collaborate with him or her on it.

If you are working on a doctoral degree and have not yet selected a topic for your dissertation, you would be wise to gauge your advisor's enthusiasm for a topic before committing to it. A doctoral dissertation is a collaboration between a student and a mentor. One of the common reasons that a dissertation is not completed is that the advisor has little interest in the topic and, consequently, does not invest very much of himself or herself in helping the student to complete it.

## Ability to Prioritize

A person can have enthusiasm for a project, but be unable to make completing it a priority. He or she might have other responsibilities that preclude doing so. It can be frustrating to have a coauthor who is unable to meet deadlines because of another responsibility to which you would also give a higher priority.

## Writing Ability and Style

It is, of course, desirable that a coauthor be able to write well. It is also desirable for his or her writing style to be similar to yours. It usually is not advantageous for a reader to be able to detect which coauthor drafted a particular paragraph.

### Knowledge and Experience

A person who lacks some of the knowledge and experience needed to meet his or her responsibilities will be a poor choice unless you are willing to give the person time to acquire these abilities.

### Expertise in Field

If you lack some of the knowledge and experience needed to do a project and do not have the time or opportunity to acquire it, this will obviously be a crucial consideration.

### Compatibility

Although it is certainly more comfortable to have collaborators who share your points of view, it might not be particularly desirable. It depends on the purpose of the project. If, for example, the project is a paper in which you intend to examine an issue from several points of view, it would certainly be desirable to have coauthors who do not share your points of view.

### Respect

A collaboration in which there is mutual respect is more likely to be successful than one in which there is not. The only reason I can think of why I would consider collaborating with someone whom I did not highly respect is that he or she could provide some difficult to obtain resources (for example, funding) that I needed to do a project.

### Willingness to Compromise

No matter how compatible your collaborators' points of view are with yours, there are almost certain to be things about which you will disagree and on which you are going to have to compromise. Some persons have an extremely difficult time doing this. They almost always become defensive when a position is questioned. It probably would not be particularly enjoyable to collaborate with such a person.

### Willingness to Negotiate

There are several issues you must resolve if you are to maximize the likelihood that a collaboration will be successful. A successful collaboration yields a publication (or publications) of which you and your coauthor(s) can be proud and does not damage or destroy your relationship with the coauthor(s). Perhaps the best way to maximize the likelihood that a collaboration will be successful is to negotiate a joint collaboration agreement with your coauthors. Some of the issues that you would negotiate in such an agreement are described in the next section.

## JOINT COLLABORATION AGREEMENTS

A joint collaboration agreement is a contract and like all contracts, it is best if it is written. An agreement for a book is likely to deal with more issues than one for a journal article. Issues that could be dealt with in a joint collaboration agreement include the following: the tasks assigned to each coauthor, how royalty income will be divided, deadlines by which tasks have to be completed as well as what happens if deadlines are not met, who has the final word on questions of content and style, how authorship will be credited (that is, whose name comes first), how disputes will be resolved (for example, by using a arbitrator from the American Arbitration Association if they cannot be resolved by the coauthors), conditions under which coauthors can and cannot use material from the joint work in other publications, and what happens to a coauthor's royalty income and authorship credit (on the title page and cover) when he or she dies or for some other reason decides not to collaborate on future revisions of a book.

If your coauthor (or coauthors) are friends, you might feel that there is no need to have a written agreement. Based on a personal experience and the comments of several authors with whom I discussed this matter, I strongly recommend that you have one. Because of the time spent negotiating the agreement, you and your coauthor(s) are likely to be more aware of your responsibilities for the project than you would have been otherwise.

Before developing a joint collaboration agreement — indeed before deciding whether to coauthor an article or book — you and your potential coauthor (or coauthors) should have a frank discussion. In it, you should provide each other with answers to questions such as:

What are my goals for doing this project?

How do I take criticism? Do I take it well if it is constructive? Do I not take it well at first, but usually do after sleeping on it? Do I sometimes tend to be overly sensitive to criticism?

How do I attack a writing project? Do I write a certain amount every day? Do I do it in a long burst just before a deadline? Do I work on it mostly during vacations or other periods when I have large blocks of time available?

How do I relate to deadlines? Do I think a deadline is a deadline and should be met exactly? Do I think that deadlines should be flexible within reason? Do I frequently miss them?

How often would I like to meet with my coauthors? Do I think we should meet on a regular basis (for example, monthly) for progress reports and to toss ideas around or only when there is something that we need to do together?

How long am I willing to devote myself to this project?

What parts of doing a writing project are most odious to me?

Where does this project stand in relation to my other priorities?

If the answers to these questions suggested that the collaboration would be likely to be successful, you and your coauthor(s) would negotiate a joint collaboration agreement. There is a model for one in Appendix B of Silverman (1998a).

# 13

# Publishing beyond Tenure

Tenure has been said to give a free ride to the lazy and those whose careers have languished. . . . A number of legislatures around the country have supported a "post-tenure review" process, in which tenured individuals would be evaluated.

— from a position paper on the faculty page of the
Auburn University web site

My primary focus throughout this book has been on publishing for tenure. Certainly, a college or university faculty member is expected to continue publishing after receiving tenure and becoming an associate professor. He or she can be penalized in several ways for not doing so. Annual salary increases for associate professors at many colleges and universities are linked to scholarly productivity. Promotion from associate to full professor at most colleges and universities also tends to require such productivity.

Until recently, once a person had tenure, he or she almost always had it for life. Post-tenure review bills had been passed or were being considered by the legislatures in a number of states when this chapter was written. A post-tenure review could cause an associate or full professor to lose tenure (and possibly be fired) if he or she ceased being productive as a scholar. Post-tenure review initiatives and their possible consequences are explored in this chapter along with some publishing opportunities that are more likely to be available to tenured than to nontenured faculty.

## POST-TENURE REVIEW

Some persons cease being productive as scholars after receiving tenure and others do so after being promoted to full professor. They do little or no research or publication and do not engage in other scholarly activities. Traditionally, what a college or university could do to rid itself of tenured faculty who have ceased being productive has been limited to denying them merit salary increases, taking away their graduate standing, or, if they are associate professors, refusing to promote them to full professors. Recent articles in the *Chronicle of Higher Education* suggest that this situation could be changing in at least a few states and could change in others if post-tenure, review-based revocation survives legal challenges. Undoubtedly, at least some academics who lose tenure on this basis will sue for its reinstatement. They could argue cogently that post-tenure review would function like an *ex post facto* law and, consequently, could not apply to faculty who have been tenured for a number of years. This argument, of course, is unlikely to be usable by faculty who do not have tenure. Consequently, present faculty who do not have tenure will have to play the publishing for tenure game throughout their academic careers.

When this chapter was written, post-tenure reviews usually resulted in a warning if scholarly productivity was found to be lacking. The threat of loss of tenure usually was sufficient to motivate those receiving such a warning to increase their productivity to an acceptable level.

## POST-TENURE PUBLISHING

You will have the same types of publishing opportunities after receiving tenure that you had before receiving it. You also might have some others, particularly if you have at least begun to establish a national reputation as an authority on a niche in your field. These could include: invited book chapters and papers for journals, textbooks, books and other materials for workshops, collaborative research with students that yields publications, and books and articles and other writings about your field for the general public. Although they are not the only such publishing opportunities, they include ones in which relatively large numbers of tenured faculty have engaged.

## Invited Book Chapters and Papers for Journals

You are likely to have at least the beginnings of a national reputation by the time you receive tenure. Consequently, you are likely to receive invitations to write chapters for books or papers for journals. Such publications are prestigious and, if well done, are likely to enhance your national (and possibly international) reputation as a scholar.

## Textbooks

Nontenured faculty are often advised to delay writing college textbooks, particularly ones for lower-division undergraduate courses, until they have received tenure. There are at least two reasons. First, some members of your promotion and tenure committee might not consider textbooks to be scholarly publications. Second, the hundreds (perhaps thousands) of hours it takes to write a textbook might not allow you sufficient time to accumulate an adequate number of publications that the members of your committee are likely to consider scholarly.

You might want to consider writing or collaborating on a college textbook after you have obtained tenure. You, your students, your institution, and your field could benefit in a number of ways from your doing so.

It would provide an opportunity to influence the attitudes of future generations of specialists in your field nationally.

If the textbook were for a course you taught, the course would probably be more innovative and up to date than otherwise. If your textbook is successful, you will probably be asked to revise it every few years, which means that you will have to be innovative (to classroom test and refine your approaches for communicating concepts) and keep up to date.

It would enhance your national reputation (assuming, of course, that it was well written). You are more likely to become well known in your field by writing textbooks than by writing journal articles.

It would enable you to directly or indirectly augment your income. Directly would be through receipt of royalty income. Indirectly could be getting larger merit salary increases than otherwise and receiving honorariums for lectures and workshops.

For information about other ways you could benefit from writing a textbook as well as practical information including how to select a publisher, prepare a proposal, and negotiate a contract, see Silverman (1998a).

### Books and Other Materials for Workshops

After you have developed a national or international reputation in your field, you are likely to be asked to present workshops on your specialty to students who are majoring in it or professionals who are employed in it. Workshops intended for professionals could be offered for continuing education credit and used to partially fulfill a requirement for license renewal.

Publications can yield workshops and workshops can yield publications. With regard to the former, the content of a workshop can be largely that of one or more articles or books you have published. With regard to the latter, the content of a workshop can be communicated in book form. This was, for example, the origin of my book *Authoring Books and Materials for Students, Academics, and Professionals* (Silverman, 1998a). I have been offering faculty-development workshops for persons who are considering writing such books and materials since the late 1980s.

You might find it advantageous to be proactive rather than reactive with regard to workshops. That is, develop one or more workshops that you would be willing to offer under the auspices of a college or other organization (possibly for continuing education credit) and market it (or them). You would receive an honorarium and travel expenses for conducting such a workshop. If a workshop were based on a book you wrote, a copy of the book could be included in the package that participants receive.

Doing such workshops can be beneficial to you in ways other than financial. It can enable you to travel at someone else's expense nationally, or possibly even internationally. Furthermore, conducting such workshops tends to be more enjoyable than teaching required college courses because people usually are there to learn rather than to meet a requirement. Finally, conducting such workshops tends to enhance both your national reputation and your status within your college or university. Few, if any, colleges or universities would try to terminate the tenure of a faculty member whose presence added to its visibility and prestige.

### Collaborative Research with Students that Yields Publications

After you obtain tenure, you probably will not have to be as concerned about contributing to publications of which you are not first author and to which your contribution was mainly a conceptual one, such as publications based on theses or dissertations that you directed. If you were engaged in a systematic program of research, you could collaborate with students on studies related to the project and have your contribution be mainly generating ideas for and helping to design them. Your contribution could also include financial support if you had a grant.

You, of course, can be a coauthor of publications with students before receiving tenure. However, doing so without being able to document that your contribution was substantial can be risky.

## Books, Articles, and Other Writings about Your Field for the General Public

After you obtain tenure, you might want to seriously consider writing books and articles about your field for the general public. Many scholars who have national or international reputations in their field have written them. So also have college faculty who do not have such a reputation, but do have the ability to write about aspects of their field in ways that are both understandable and interesting to persons who are not knowledgeable about the field.

There are a number of possible types of articles or books that you might consider writing.

Articles or books that describe some research or theory from your field in a way that is likely to be both understandable and interesting to persons outside of your field. The intended audience could be either children or adults. Albert Einstein and Stephen Hawking, for example, wrote such books.

Articles or books that are intended to benefit, not merely inform, the reader. Included here would be self-help and do-it-yourself books. A professor of speech-language pathology, for example, might write a self-help book for people who stutter. A professor of law might write a do-it-yourself book for drafting simple wills.

Novels and docu-novels. Professors in a number of fields, including my own, have written novels and docu-novels about them. By a docu-novel I mean one that relates an actual incident (or incidents) in a novel format. Although some of the characters and dialogue are fictionalized, the descriptions of important events are accurate. Many of James Michener's novels are of this type.

Poetry. Although it is less usual for scholars to write poetry than the other types of writing mentioned thus far, some have done so. In my field, for example, poetry has been used to convey how it feels to have a speech or hearing disorder.

Documentary film (videotape) scripts. Although film, like poetry, is not a
    medium for which large numbers of academic authors have written, some
    have done so. Their films have appeared on educational TV channels.

These are intended merely to be suggestions. There undoubtedly are other
types of writing for the general public that it would be both appropriate
and helpful for a professor to do.

# 14

## They Rejected It! Now What?

We have read your manuscript with boundless delight. If we were to publish your paper, it would be impossible for us to publish any work of lower standard. And as it is unthinkable that in the next thousand years we shall see its equal, we are, to our regret, compelled to return your divine composition, and to beg you a thousand times to overlook our short sight and timidity.

— rejection slip from a Chinese economic journal,
quoted in Burnham (1994, p. 162)

This chapter was frankly an afterthought. When I was close to finishing the manuscript for this book, I came upon a book by Sophy Burnham, entitled *For Writers Only*, on the remainder table at my local Barnes & Noble bookstore. The book contains a collection of inspiring thoughts on various aspects of being a writer. One aspect was coping with a manuscript being rejected. Reading the comments about dealing with rejection brought to mind a colleague who wanted to be a scholar and had the ability to be a good one. He was demoralized that his first journal article was rejected (judging by comments he made to me). He never again attempted to publish another. A contributor — perhaps the main one — to his becoming demoralized was making an erroneous assumption.

There are at least three erroneous assumptions you could make about the review process for journal articles and books that could cause you to become demoralized.

## IF A MANUSCRIPT OR PROPOSAL IS GOOD, IT WILL BE ACCEPTED

Publishable manuscripts and proposals for them frequently get rejected. It is good fortune, rather than the norm, to have a publishable manuscript or a proposal for one accepted by the first publisher to which it is submitted. This is even true for books that became best sellers. According to Burnham (1994, p. 155),

Robert Pirsig received 121 rejections, he says, before *Zen and the Art of Motorcycle Maintenance* was accepted for publication. *Jonathan Livingston Seagull* circulated to forty publishers. Norman Mailer's *The Naked and the Dead* went to eleven publishers before the twelfth dared accept it. Joseph Heller's classic *Catch-22*, William Kennedy's *Ironweed*, Erich Segal's *Love Story*, Tom Clancy's *The Hunt for Red October*, *The Diary of Anne Frank*, or M. Scott Peck's *The Road Less Traveled* . . . so many manuscripts circulating valiantly to one publisher after another before rushing off to stardom.

Consequently, it is not the greatest idea for preserving your mental health to assume that if a manuscript or proposal is good the first editor to whom it is submitted will accept it. Be thankful if he or she accepts it, but do not become demoralized if it is not accepted.

## IF A MANUSCRIPT OR PROPOSAL IS REJECTED BY ONE PUBLISHER, IT IS UNLIKELY TO BE ACCEPTED BY ANOTHER

If a journal article or book contains information that can be used by at least a few people, this assumption is highly unlikely to be valid. A manuscript or proposal that is well crafted and contains useful information that does not appeal to one editor is likely to appeal to another. This is why literary agents do not become discouraged by rejections and keep circulating book proposals for which they believe there is a market. It can take more than 100 submissions to find an editor to which a book manuscript or proposal appeals. The proposal for my one trade book was rejected by an acquisitions editor at more than 20 publishers before being submitted to an acquisitions editor to which it appealed. Some of my journal articles were rejected by the first journal to which they were submitted. The acquisitions editor for a large publisher rejected a proposal for one of my college textbooks. He left and his replacement liked the proposal and offered a contract. Persistence is likely to pay off if a manuscript or proposal is well crafted and contains useful information.

## MANUSCRIPTS ARE USUALLY ACCEPTED FOR PUBLICATION AS IS

Perhaps one of the worst things that can happen to you is to have the first manuscript or proposal you submit for publication accepted essentially as is. You would tend to become discouraged when subsequent ones were not accepted essentially as is. Few journal articles or book proposals are accepted without changes being requested. Almost any manuscript or proposal can be improved. A lack of suggestions for changes probably is more likely to reflect disinterest on the part of the editor and reviewers than that the manuscript or proposal is perfect.

If you require further evidence, I suggest that you read a book by James Michener, entitled *James A. Michener's Writer's Handbook*, that was published in 1992. In it, Michener includes copies of editors' comments and requests for changes for one of his books. Receiving such comments and reviews would probably devastate most academic authors who did not realize that this is the way the publishing game is played.

## ALLOW YOURSELF TO GRIEVE

Rejection always results in a loss. When a person sustains a loss, it is normal for him or her to grieve. Even if you do not make any of the assumptions about publishing that were mentioned, you will still have to go through the grieving process whenever you have a manuscript or proposal rejected. You will experience disbelief, anger, and depression. This is normal, and you should not try to avoid experiencing these feelings. To do so can cause stress that can be harmful to you both physiologically and psychologically. However, as soon as you can after having a manuscript or proposal rejected, make whatever changes you think are necessary and submit it to another publisher.

# References

AGNEW, N. M., & PYKE, S. W. (1975). *The Science Game*. Englewood Cliffs, NJ: Prentice-Hall.

ALLISON, A., & FRONGIA, T. (Eds.) (1992). *The Grad Student's Guide to Getting Published*. New York, NY: Prentice-Hall.

BENNETT, H. Z., & LARSEN, M. (1988). *How to Write with a Collaborator*. Cincinnati, OH: Writer's Digest Books.

BLUE, M. (1990). *By the Book: Legal ABCs for the Printed Word*. Flagstaff, AZ: Northland Publishing Company.

BUNNIN, B., & BEREN, P. (1988). *The Writer's Legal Companion*. Reading, MA: Addison-Wesley.

BURNHAM, S. (1994). *For Writers Only*. New York, NY: Ballantine Books.

CANTOR, J. A. (1993). *A Guide to Academic Writing*. Westport, CT: Greenwood Press.

CAPLOW, T., & MCGEE, R. J. (1958). *The Academic Marketplace*. New York, NY: Basic Books.

CHICKERING, R. B., & HARTMAN, M. S. (1987). *How to Register a Copyright and Protect Your Creative Work*. New York, NY: Charles Scribner's Sons.

DIBLE, D. M. (1978). *What Everybody Should Know about Patents, Trademarks, and Copyrights*. Fairfield, CA: Entrepreneur Press.

FIEGL, H. (1953). The scientific outlook: Naturalism and humanism. In Herbert Fiegl and May Brodbeck (Eds.), *Readings in the Philosophy of Science*. New York, NY: Appleton-Century-Crofts, 8–18.

*Fields' Reference Book for Non-sexist Words and Phrases* (1987). Raleigh, NC.: Fields' Enterprises.

GLASSER, W. (1976). *Positive Addiction*. New York, NY: Harper & Row.

*Guidelines for Bias-Free Publishing*. (n.d.). Hightstown, NJ: McGraw-Hill.

HARNAD, S. (November 11, 1991). Scientific skywriting and the prepublication continuum of scientific inquiry. *Current Contents*, 45, 9–13.

JASSIN, L. J., & SCHECHTER, S. C. (1998). *The Copyright Permission and Libel Handbook: A Step-by-Step Guide for Writers, Editors, and Publishers*. New York, NY: John Wiley & Sons.

KEYES, R. (1995). *The Courage to Write*. New York, NY: Henry Holt.

KING, L. S. (1991). *Why Not Say It Clearly: A Guide to Expository Writing*. Boston, MA: Little, Brown & Company.

KNIGHT, L. W. (1988). Seeking federal funding for research. In A. Leigh Deneef, Craufurd D. Goodwin, & Ellen Stern McCrate (Eds.), *The Academic's Handbook*. Durham, NC: Duke University Press, 175–186.

KORZYBSKI, A. (1958). *Science and Sanity: An Introduction to Non-Aristotelian Systems and General Semantics* (Fourth Edition). Lakeville, CT: Institute of General Semantics.

KOZAK, E. M. (1990). *Every Writer's Guide to Copyright and Publishing Law*. New York, NY: Henry Holt.

KREMENTZ, J. (1996). *The Writer's Desk*. New York, NY: Random House.

LUEY, B. (1987). *Handbook for Academic Authors*. New York, NY: Cambridge University Press.

MICHENER, J. A. (1992). *James A. Michener's Writer's Handbook*. New York, NY: Random House.

MILLER, C., & SWIFT, K. (1988). *The Handbook of Nonsexist Writing*. New York, NY: Harper & Row.

NOVICK, K. P., & CHASEN, J. S. (1984). *The Rights of Authors and Artists*. New York, NY: Bantam Books.

PARSONS, P. (1989). *Getting Published: The Acquisition Process at University Presses*. Knoxville, TN: University of Tennessee Press.

PENNER, M. J., & BILGER, R. C. (1989). Adaptation and the masking of tinnitus. *Journal of Speech and Hearing Research*, 32, 339–346.

*Principles of Good Writing* (1969). Westport, CT: Famous Writers School.

RADIL-WEISS, T. (1983). Men in extreme conditions: Some medical and psychological aspects of the Auschwitz Concentration Camp. *Psychiatry*, 46, 259–268.

SILVERMAN, F. H. (1998a). *Authoring Books and Materials for Students, Academics, and Professionals*. Westport, CT: Praeger.

SILVERMAN, F. H. (1998b). *Research Design and Evaluation in Speech-Language Pathology and Audiology* (Fourth Edition). Boston, MA: Allyn & Bacon.

SILVERMAN, F. H., & WILLIAMS, D. E. (1973). Use of revision by elementary-school stutterers and nonstutterers during oral reading. *Journal of*

*Speech and Hearing Research*, 16, 584–585.

STRONG, W. S. (1984). *The Copyright Book: A Practical Guide* (Second Edition). Cambridge, MA: MIT Press.

STRUNK, W., & WHITE, E. B. (1979). *The Elements of Style* (Third Edition). New York, NY: Macmillian.

VAN TIL, W. (1986). *Writing for Professional Publication* (Second Edition). Boston, MA: Allyn & Bacon.

ZINSSER, W. (1988). *Writing to Learn*. New York, NY: Harper & Row.

# Index

## ABOUT THE AUTHOR

**Franklin H. Silverman** is Professor of Speech Pathology at Marquette University and Clinical Professor of Rehabilitation Medicine at the Medical College of Wisconsin. He has written more than a dozen texts or professional books including *Authoring Books and Materials for Students, Academics, and Professionals* (Praeger, 1998) and more than 125 articles in professional journals. He is a past president of the Text and Academic Authors Association and has served as an Associate Editor of the *Journal of Speech and Hearing Research.*